Pat Sloan

WHaT a NoVeL iDea!

12 QUICK QUILTS FROM NOVELTY FABRICS

LEISURE ARTS, INC.
Little Rock, Arkansas

EDITORIAL STAFF

Editor-in-Chief: Susan White Sullivan
Quilt Publications Director: Cheryl Johnson
Special Projects Director: Susan Frantz Wiles
Senior Prepress Director: Mark Hawkins
Art Publications Director: Rhonda Shelby
Technical Writer: Jean Lewis
Associate Editor: Lisa Lancaster
Editorial Writer: Susan McManus Johnson
Art Category Manager: Lora Puls
Graphic Artists: Jacob Casleton, Becca Snider, and Amy Temple
Imaging Technician: Stephanie Johnson
Prepress Technician: Janie Marie Wright
Photography Manager: Katherine Laughlin
Contributing Photographers: Mark Mathews and Ken West
Publishing Systems Administrator: Becky Riddle
Mac Information Technology Specialist: Robert Young

BUSINESS STAFF

President and Chief Executive Officer: Rick Barton
Vice President and Chief Operations Officer: Tom Siebenmorgen
Vice President of Sales: Mike Behar
Director of Finance and Administration: Laticia Mull Dittrich
National Sales Director: Martha Adams
Creative Services: Chaska Lucas
Information Technology Director: Hermine Linz
Controller: Francis Caple
Vice President, Operations: Jim Dittrich
Retail Customer Service Manager: Stan Raynor
Print Production Manager: Fred F. Pruss

Library of Congress Control Number: 2010942736
• ISBN-13: 978-1-60900-002-8

Contents

My love affair with novelty fabrics started early—like on my first quilt! When I took my beginner's class I was drawn to a fabric printed with figures. For my second quilt? Apples! From there, it became an adventure to collect and use novelty prints.

With this book, I want to share a few pointers and opinions to help you use and enjoy your novelty prints. You'll find twelve simple quilts designed to showcase the fun fabrics. There's also a quick pillow design you can make to feature a novelty print of any size.

After 18 years of quilting, I still find novelty prints to be full of humor and beauty. They tell a story as no other fabric can. Have fun discovering the stories—and the quilts—in your novelty fabrics!

—Pat

Meet Pat Sloan

You'll never meet a more devoted fan of the quilting arts than Pat Sloan! When she isn't designing fabric, writing quilt books, teaching quilt techniques, or developing patterns, she draws on her background as a computer programmer to maintain her popular Web site and blog at PatSloan.com. Pat's joyful approach to quilting seems to be contagious, because "Sloanies" (as Pat's devoted fans call themselves) love to keep up with their favorite designer while she pursues the quilting life with a passion.

"I've been fulltime as a quilt designer and teacher since 2000," says Pat, "with my husband Gregg handling the business side of managing our company. My life is all about quilting, twenty-four/seven."

If you want to discover more of Pat's exciting designs and original quilt-making techniques, visit your local fabric store or LeisureArts.com to collect all of her books!

Novelty Prints

What are Novelty prints?

Novelty prints are fabrics printed with easily recognizable motifs. Animals, holidays, sports, food, and transportation are just a few of the numerous themes available.

Sometimes referred to as conversation prints, novelty prints first became fashionable during the late 1800s. Small-scale motifs such as horseshoes and anchors were popular themes for adult and children's clothing.

In the 1930s, manufacturers began to sell assorted "dry goods" in fabric sacks printed with appealing novelty prints. Homemakers then used the empty sacks to make clothing and quilts.

During the 1940s, 50s and 60s, in addition to the cute generic motifs, branding became immensely popular. Product-related logos, and movie and cartoon characters appeared.

The popularity of novelty prints continues today. The variety seems to be endless and includes just about any theme you can imagine. No longer used just for clothing and bedding, novelty print fabrics are a favorite with quilters.

About Novelty Prints

Depending on the number, placement, and size of the motifs, each novelty print can have its own distinctive look.

- A fabric might contain several poses or views of the same motif. In Fig. 1 a single sock monkey appears in different poses.

- There may be different images of the same *type* of motif, such as the dogs shown in Fig. 2.

- The size of motifs can vary from small, like the flags in Fig. 3, to very large like the sailboats in Fig. 4.

Fig. 1

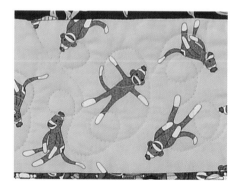

Fig. 2

Fig. 3

Fig. 4

- Motifs can be "tossed" on the background, making the fabric non-directional as shown in Figs. 1 and 5, or they may be directional as in Fig. 6.

- Novelty prints can be part of a line of fabrics. There are three fabrics from the same line in All Aboard!, page 14.

Fig. 5

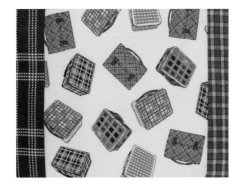

Fig. 6

Collecting and Buying Novelty Prints

While the project instructions in this book list fabric requirements for each quilt, some quilters like to collect novelty prints without a particular project in mind. If you're one of those, here are some suggestions for building a collection.

- Purchase novelty prints from each location you visit on vacation. You can use these pieces to make a memory quilt of your trip.

- Start with a theme that calls to you. You might collect images of your favorite things, such as cupcakes, animals, or coffee mugs.

- Collect novelty prints that remind you of events or people in your life. The chair print in Let's Go Camping, page 46, brings to mind my Nana's porch chairs.

Now comes the question that I am asked all the time—how much to buy?

- If you are collecting every bug (or fruit or cat, etc.) print you see in hopes of making a scrappy sampler quilt someday, then I suggest you buy a $1/4$ yard or fat quarter.

- If it is a large print you might want to fussy cut, like the trains in All Aboard!, page 14, or one that might work for sashings, like the brown print in Monkey Business, page 52, I recommend buying at least $1/2$ to 1 yard.

- If a certain fabric makes your heart race, makes you smile, or would be perfect for borders, purchase at least $1^1/2$ yards for a wall hanging and 4 yards for a bed-size quilt. I have been known to buy 5 yards of a print I love—really, it's true!

Now let's get started making a quilt!

A Pair of Winners

Version 1

I was really tickled by the award ribbons, the cute retro appearance of the ducks, and the funky trees in these novelty prints! It was a case of "had to have them!" For this quilt, I used almost all the prints in the fabric line. Many of the prints are directional, so the quilt design needed to allow for that and show the prints to their best advantage. Of course, you don't have to use only fabrics from the same line. Just choose any large prints that work well together. They'll look great.

Finished Size: 63$^1/_2$" x 73" (161 cm x 185 cm)
Finished Block Size: 9$^1/_2$" x 9$^1/_2$" (24 cm x 24 cm)

Fabric Requirements

Yardage is based on 43"/44" (109 cm/112 cm) wide fabric. A pre-cut bundle of 10" fabric squares called a Layer Cake works well for this project or you can cut squares from assorted novelty prints.

- 1 novelty print Layer Cake or 30 assorted novelty print squares 10" x 10" (25 cm x 25 cm)
- $^1/_4$ yd (23 cm) of white tone-on-tone print (block "ribbons")
- $^1/_4$ yd (23 cm) of light green tone-on-tone print (block "ribbons")
- $^3/_8$ yd (34 cm) of green tone-on-tone print (middle border)
- 2 yds (1.8 m) of orange print (inner and outer borders)
- $^5/_8$ yd (57 cm) of orange tone-on-tone print (block "ribbons" and binding)
- 4$^1/_2$ yds (4.1 m) of fabric for backing

You will also need:
- 71$^1/_2$" x 81" (182 cm x 206 cm) piece of batting

Cutting the Pieces

Follow Rotary Cutting, page 71, to cut fabric. Cut all strips from the selvage-to-selvage width of the fabric. Cutting lengths for borders are exact. All measurements include 1/4" seam allowances.

Tip: Noting that some prints may be directional, arrange your squares on a design wall or large flat surface before cutting until you are pleased with the placement of the squares.

From *each* novelty print square:
- Keeping the orientation of the prints the same as your design wall arrangement, cut 2 **large rectangles** 4½" x 10".

From white tone-on-tone print:
- Cut 3 strips 2" wide. From these strips, cut 10 **small squares** 2" x 2" and 20 **small rectangles** 2" x 4½".

From light green tone-on-tone print:
- Cut 3 strips 2" wide. From these strips, cut 10 **small squares** 2" x 2" and 20 **small rectangles** 2" x 4½".

From green tone-on-tone print:
- Cut 2 side middle borders 1½" x 61½", piecing as necessary.
- Cut 2 top/bottom middle borders 1½" x 54", piecing as necessary.

From orange print:
- Cut 2 *lengthwise* side inner borders 2½" x 57½".
- Cut 2 *lengthwise* top/bottom inner borders 2½" x 52".
- Cut 2 *lengthwise* side outer borders 5" x 63½".
- Cut 2 *lengthwise* top/bottom outer borders 5" x 63".

From orange tone-on-tone print:
- Cut 3 strips 2" wide. From these strips, cut 10 **small squares** 2" x 2" and 20 **small rectangles** 2" x 4½".
- Cut 8 **binding strips** 1½" wide.

Making the Blocks

*Follow **Piecing**, page 71, and **Pressing**, page 72, to make the Blocks. Match right sides and use ¼" seam allowances throughout. For each block you will need 2 same-fabric small rectangles, 1 contrasting small square, and 2 same-fabric large rectangles.*

1. Matching short edges, sew 2 **small rectangles** and 1 **small square** together to make Unit 1. Make 30 Unit 1's.

2. Matching long edges, sew 2 **large rectangles** and 1 Unit 1 together to make Block. Make 30 Blocks.

Assembling the Quilt Top

*Refer to **Quilt Top Diagram** for placement.*

1. Sew 3 Blocks with vertical Unit 1's and 2 Blocks with horizontal Unit 1's together to make Row 1. Make 3 Row 1's.

2. Sew 2 Blocks with vertical Unit 1's and 3 Blocks with horizontal Unit 1's together to make Row 2. Make 3 Row 2's.

3. Alternating Rows 1 and 2, sew Rows together to make **quilt top center**.

Adding the Borders

1. Matching centers and corners, sew **side** then **top/bottom inner borders** to quilt top center.

2. Matching centers and corners, sew **side** then **top/bottom middle borders** to quilt top center.

3. Matching centers and corners, sew **side** then **top/bottom outer borders** to quilt top center to complete Quilt Top.

Completing the Quilt

1. Follow **Quilting**, page 72, to mark, layer, and quilt as desired. My quilt is machine quilted with loops and circles in the small rectangles of the blocks and in the inner and outer borders. There is a large wave pattern in the large rectangles of the blocks and a small wave in the middle border.

2. Refer to **Adding A Hanging Sleeve**, page 76, to make and attach a hanging sleeve, if desired.

3. Follow **Binding**, page 76, to bind quilt using **binding strips**. ✳

Unit 1 (make 30)

Block (make 30)

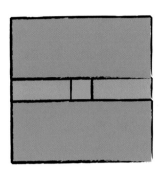

Quilt Top Diagram

Row 1 (make 3)

Row 2 (make 3)

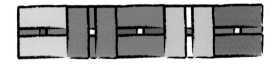

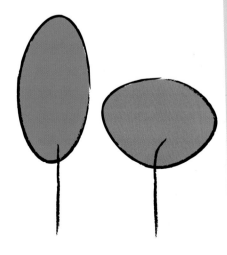

A Pair of Winners

Version 2

Finished Size: 39" x 39" (99 cm x 99 cm)
Finished Block Size: 9¹/₂" x 9¹/₂" (24 cm x 24 cm)

Fabric Requirements

Yardage is based on 43"/44" (109 cm/112 cm) wide fabric. A pre-cut bundle of 10" fabric squares called a Layer Cake works well for this project or you can cut squares from assorted novelty prints.

- 1 novelty print Layer Cake or 16 assorted novelty print squares 10" x 10" (25 cm x 25 cm)
- ¹/₄ yd (23 cm) of green tone-on-tone print (block "ribbons")
- ¹/₄ yd (23 cm) of brown tone-on-tone print (block "ribbons")
- ¹/₄ yd (23 cm) of red tone-on-tone print (binding)
- 2⁵/₈ yds (2.4 m) of fabric for backing

You will also need:
- 47" x 47" (119 cm x 119 cm) piece of batting

Cutting the Pieces

Follow **Rotary Cutting***, page 71, to cut fabric. Cut all strips from the selvage-to-selvage width of the fabric. All measurements include* 1/4" *seam allowances.*

Tip: Noting that some prints may be directional, arrange your squares on a design wall or large flat surface before cutting until you are pleased with the placement of the squares.

From *each* novelty print square:
- Keeping the orientation of the prints the same as your design wall arrangement, cut 2 **large rectangles** 4$\frac{1}{2}$" x 10".

From green tone-on-tone print:
- Cut 6 **small squares** 2" x 2" and 20 **small rectangles** 2" x 4$\frac{1}{2}$".

From brown tone-on-tone print:
- Cut 10 **small squares** 2" x 2" and 12 **small rectangles** 2" x 4$\frac{1}{2}$".

From red tone-on-tone print:
- Cut 5 **binding strips** 1$\frac{1}{2}$" wide.

Making the Blocks
1. Follow **Making The Blocks**, page 8, to make 16 Blocks.

Assembling the Quilt Top
Refer to **Quilt Top Diagram** *for placement.*

1. Sew 2 Blocks with vertical Unit 1's and 2 Blocks with horizontal Unit 1's together to make Row. Make 4 Rows.

2. Alternating orientation, sew Rows together to complete Quilt Top.

Completing the Quilt
1. Follow **Quilting**, page 72, to mark, layer, and quilt as desired. My quilt is machine quilted with loops and circles in the small rectangles of the blocks and a large wave pattern in the block rectangles.

2. Refer to **Adding A Hanging Sleeve**, page 76, to make and attach a hanging sleeve, if desired.

3. Follow **Binding**, page 76, to bind quilt using **binding strips**. ❀

Block (make 16)

Row (make 4)

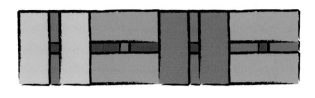

Quilt Top Diagram

54x54
6x6   5x5 +6"border

All Aboard!

I think this train fabric is some of the nicest I've seen. The image in the block on the top right makes me want to buy a big white hat and a train case so I can ride the Orient Express! I used 3 different novelty fabrics in this quilt. You could easily do the block centers with many prints, so the design is very versatile. Grab some fabric—we're about to leave the station!

Finished Size: 55" x 68" (140 cm x 173 cm)
Finished Block Size: 12" x 12" (30 cm x 30 cm)

Fabric Requirements
Yardage is based on 43"/44" (109 cm/112 cm) wide fabric.

$^5/_8$ yd (57 cm) **each** of 2 novelty prints (blocks)

1 yd (91 cm) of novelty print #3 (outer border)

$1^5/_8$ yds (1.5 m) of gold tone-on-tone print (blocks and sashings)

$1^1/_8$ yds (1 m) **total** of assorted green prints (blocks and sashing squares)

$^3/_4$ yd (69 cm) of dark purple print (middle borders, outer border sashings, and binding)

$4^1/_4$ yds (3.9 m) of fabric for backing

You will also need:

63" x 76" (160 cm x 193 cm) rectangle of batting

Cutting the Pieces

Follow Rotary Cutting, page 71, to cut fabric. Cut all strips from the selvage-to-selvage width of the fabric. Cutting lengths for borders are exact. All measurements include 1/4" seam allowances.

From each of 2 novelty prints:
- Cut 6 large squares 8½" x 8½".

From novelty print #3:
- Cut 6 strips 6½" wide. From these strips, cut 6 short rectangles 6½" x 12½" and 8 long rectangles 6½" x 13½".

From gold tone-on-tone print:
- Cut 8 strips 3" wide. From these strips, cut 104 medium squares 3" x 3".
- Cut 4 strips 2½" wide. From these strips, cut 64 small squares 2½" x 2½".
- Cut 6 strips 1½" wide. From these strips, cut 17 sashing strips 1½" x 12½".
- Cut 2 top/bottom inner borders 1½" x 38½".
- Cut 2 side inner borders 1½" x 53½", piecing as necessary.

From assorted green prints:
- Cut 152 medium squares 3" x 3".
- Cut 4 small squares 2½" x 2½".
- Cut 6 sashing squares 1½" x 1½".

From dark purple print:
- Cut 2 top/bottom middle borders 1½" x 40½", piecing as necessary.
- Cut 2 side middle borders 1½" x 55½", piecing as necessary.
- Cut 3 strips 1½" wide. From these strips, cut 18 border sashing strips 1½" x 6½".
- Cut 7 binding strips 1½" wide.

Making the Blocks

Follow Piecing, page 71, and Pressing, page 72, to make the Blocks. Match right sides and use 1/4" seam allowances throughout.

1. Place 1 green **medium square** on each corner of 1 **large square**. Stitch diagonally across each medium square; trim 1/4" from stitching line (Fig. 1). Press open to make Unit 1. Make 12 Unit 1's.

2. Draw a diagonal line on wrong side of each gold **medium square**. With right sides together, place 1 marked gold medium square on top of 1 green **medium square**. Stitch 1/4" from each side of drawn line (Fig. 2).

3. Cut along drawn line and press seam allowances toward darker fabric to make 2 Triangle-Squares. Trim each Triangle-Square to 2½" x 2½". Make 208 Triangle-Squares.

4. Sew 2 gold **small squares** and 4 Triangle-Squares together to make Unit 2. Make 24 Unit 2's.

5. Sew 4 Triangle-Squares together to make Unit 3. Make 24 Unit 3's.

6. Sew 1 Unit 1, 2 Unit 2's and 2 Unit 3's together to make Star Block A. Make 12 Star Block A's.

7. Sew 4 gold small squares, 1 green **small square**, and 4 Triangle-Squares together to make Star Block B. Make 4 Star Block B's.

Fig. 1

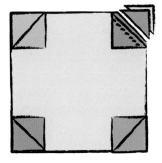

Unit 1 (make 12)

Fig. 2

Triangle-Square (make 208)

Unit 2 (make 24)

Unit 3 (make 24)

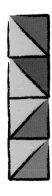

Star Block A (make 12)

Star Block B (make 4)

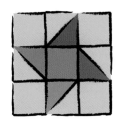

Row (make 4)

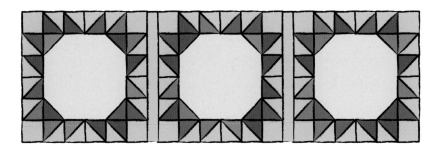

Sashing Row (make 3)

Side Outer Border (make 2)

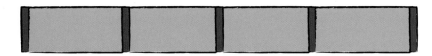

Top/Bottom Outer Border (make 2)

AsseMbling the Quilt Top

*Refer to **Quilt Top Diagram** for placement.*

1. Sew 3 Star Block A's and 2 **sashing strips** together to make Row. Make 4 Rows.

2. Sew 3 sashing strips and 2 **sashing squares** together to make Sashing Row. Make 3 sashing rows.

3. Sew Rows and sashing rows together to make **quilt top center**.

Adding the Borders

1. Matching centers and corners, sew **top/bottom** then **side inner borders** to quilt top center.

2. Matching centers and corners, sew **top/bottom** then **side middle borders** to quilt top center.

3. Sew 2 **long rectangles**, 2 **short rectangles**, and 5 **border sashing strips** together to make Side Outer Border. Make 2 side outer borders.

4. Sew 1 **short rectangle**, 2 **long rectangles**, 4 **border sashing strips**, and 2 Star Block B's together to make Top/Bottom Outer Border. Make 2 top/bottom outer borders.

5. Matching centers and corners, sew **side** then **top/bottom outer borders** to quilt top center to complete Quilt Top.

Completing the Quilt

1. Follow **Quilting**, page 72, to mark, layer, and quilt as desired. My quilt is machine quilted with outline quilting around Star Blocks A and B. There is meandering quilting in the center of each Star Block A, the gold background, and outer border rectangles. There is a wave quilted through the center of the middle border and outer border sashings.

2. Refer to **Adding A Hanging Sleeve**, page 76, to make and attach a hanging sleeve, if desired.

3. Follow **Binding**, page 76, to bind quilt using **binding strips**. ✳

Quilt Top Diagram

Churn Dash

Version 1

When I first started to collect novelty fabrics, I wanted a fun and easy way to show them off. As it happens, I've had a life-long love of the Churn Dash block. I made these two quilts a long time ago, but they are still an effective display for novelty prints. There are different novelty fabrics in each block of this quilt, but just one fabric forms the backgrounds of all the blocks and the border of Churn Dash Version 2, page 24.

Finished Size: 49" x 49" (124 cm x 124 cm)
Finished Block Size: 12" x 12" (30 cm x 30 cm)

Fabric Requirements

Yardage is based on 43"/44" (109 cm/112 cm) wide fabric.
- $^1/_4$ yd (23 cm) or 1 fat quarter of *each* of 16 novelty prints (blocks)*
- $^1/_4$ yd (23 cm) or 1 fat quarter of *each* of 16 assorted prints (blocks)*
- $^3/_8$ yd (34 cm) of fabric for binding
- $3^1/_4$ yds (3 m) of fabric for backing

You will also need:
- 57" x 57" (145 cm x 145 cm) square of batting

*A fat quarter is approximately 21" x 18" (53 cm x 46 cm).

Cutting the Pieces

Follow Rotary Cutting, page 71, to cut fabric. Cut all strips from the selvage-to-selvage width of the fabric. All measurements include ¹/₄" seam allowances.

From *each* novelty print:
- Cut 2 large squares 5" x 5".
- Cut 1 small square 4¹/₂" x 4¹/₂".
- Cut 1 strip 2¹/₂" x 21".

From *each* assorted print:
- Cut 2 large squares 5" x 5".
- Cut 1 strip 2¹/₂" x 21".

From fabric for binding:
- Cut 6 binding strips 1¹/₂" wide.

Making the blocks

*Follow **Piecing**, page 71, and **Pressing**, page 72, to make the Blocks. Match right sides and use ¹/₄" seam allowances throughout.*

1. To make 1 block, select 2 **large squares** and 1 **strip** from one assorted print. Select 2 **large squares**, 1 **strip**, and 1 **small square** from 1 novelty print.

2. Draw a diagonal line on wrong side of each novelty print **large square**. With right sides together, place 1 marked novelty print large square on top of 1 assorted print large square. Stitch ¹/₄" from each side of drawn line (Fig. 1).

3. Cut along drawn line and press seam allowances toward darker fabric to make 2 Triangle-Squares. Trim each Triangle-Square to 4¹/₂" x 4¹/₂". Make 4 Triangle-Squares.

4. Sew 1 assorted and 1 novelty print **strip** together to make Strip Set. Cut across Strip Set at 4¹/₂" intervals to make Unit 1. Make 4 Unit 1's.

5. Sew 2 Triangle-Squares and 1 Unit 1 together to make Unit 2. Make 2 Unit 2's.

6. Sew 2 Unit 1's and **small square** together to make Unit 3.

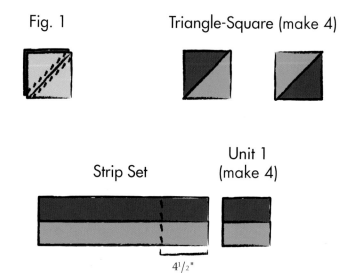

Fig. 1   Triangle-Square (make 4)

Strip Set   Unit 1 (make 4)

4¹/₂"

Unit 2 (make 2)

Unit 3

7. Sew 2 Unit's 2 and Unit 3 together to make Churn Dash Block.

8. Repeat Steps 1-7 to make 16 Churn Dash Blocks.

Assembling the Quilt Top

Refer to **Quilt Top Diagram** *for placement.*

1. Sew 4 Churn Dash Blocks together to make Row. Make 4 Rows.

2. Sew Rows together to make Quilt Top.

Completing the Quilt

1. Follow **Quilting**, page 72, to mark, layer, and quilt as desired. My quilt is machine quilted with diagonal crosshatch quilting spaced approximately 3" apart.

2. Refer to **Adding A Hanging Sleeve**, page 76, to make and attach a hanging sleeve, if desired.

3. Follow **Pat's Binding**, page 76, to bind quilt using **binding strips**. ✳

Churn Dash Block (make 16)

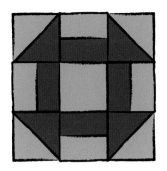

Row (make 4)

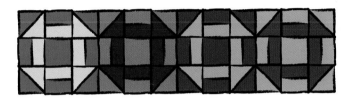

Quilt Top Diagram

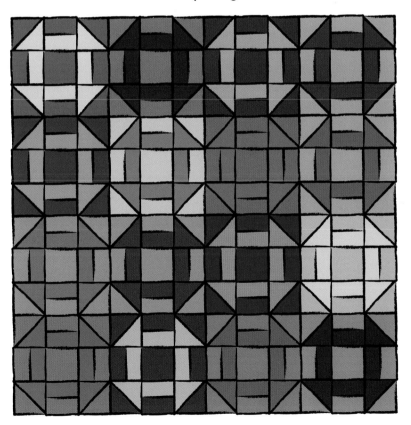

Churn Dash

Version 2

Finished Size: 36" x 36" (91 cm x 91 cm)
Finished Block Size: 9" x 9" (23 cm x 23 cm)

Fabric Requirements

Yardage is based on 43"/44" (109 cm/112 cm) wide fabric.

- $1^1/_8$ yds (1 m) of novelty print (blocks and outer border)
- $^1/_8$ yd (11 cm) *each* of 5 assorted prints (blocks)
- $^1/_4$ yd (23 cm) *each* of 3 assorted prints (blocks and binding)
- $^3/_8$ yd (34 cm) of 1 assorted print (blocks and inner border)
- $1^1/_4$ yds (1.1 m) of fabric for backing

You will also need:

- 44" x 44" (112 cm x 112 cm) square of batting

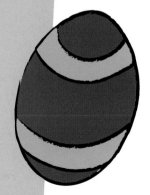

25

Cutting the Pieces

Follow Rotary Cutting, page 71, to cut fabric. Cut all strips from the selvage-to-selvage width of the fabric. Cutting lengths for borders are exact. All measurements include $1/4$" seam allowances.

From novelty print:

- Cut 2 strips 4" wide. From these strips, cut 18 **large squares** 4" x 4".
- Cut 1 strip $3^1/2$" wide. From this strip, cut 9 **small squares** $3^1/2$" x $3^1/2$".
- Cut 2 side outer borders $3^1/2$" x $29^1/2$".
- Cut 2 top/bottom outer borders $3^1/2$" x $35^1/2$".
- Cut 9 strips 2" x 16".

From *each* of 5 assorted prints:

- Cut 1 strip 4" wide. From this strip, cut 2 **large squares** 4" x 4" and 1 strip 2" x 16".

From *each* of 3 assorted prints:

- Cut 1 strip 4" wide. From this strip, cut 2 **large squares** 4" x 4" and 1 strip 2" x 16".
- Cut 1 **binding strip** $1^1/2$" x 56", piecing as necessary.

From 1 assorted print:

- Cut 1 strip 4" wide. From this strip, cut 2 **large squares** 4" x 4" and 1 strip 2" x 16".
- Cut 2 side inner borders $1^1/2$" x $27^1/2$".
- Cut 2 top/bottom inner borders $1^1/2$" x $29^1/2$".

Making the Blocks

*Follow **Piecing**, page 71, and **Pressing**, page 72, to make the Blocks. Match right sides and use $1/4$" seam allowances throughout.*

1. To make 1 block, select 2 **large squares** and 1 **strip** from one assorted print. Select 2 **large squares**, 1 **strip**, and 1 **small square** from novelty print.

2. Draw a diagonal line on wrong side of each novelty print **large square**. With right sides together, place 1 marked novelty print large square on top of 1 assorted print large square. Stitch $1/4$" from each side of drawn line (Fig. 1).

3. Cut along drawn line and press seam allowances toward darker fabric to make 2 Triangle-Squares. Trim each Triangle-Square to $3^1/2$" x $3^1/2$". Make 4 Triangle-Squares.

4. Sew 1 assorted and 1 novelty print **strip** together to make Strip Set. Cut across Strip Set at $3^1/2$" intervals to make Unit 1. Make 4 Unit 1's.

5. Sew 2 Triangle-Squares and 1 Unit 1 together to make Unit 2. Make 2 Unit 2's.

6. Sew 2 Unit 1's and **small square** together to make Unit 3.

7. Sew 2 Unit 2's and Unit 3 together to make Churn Dash Block.

8. Repeat Steps 1-7 to make 9 Churn Dash Blocks.

Assembling the Quilt Top

*Refer to **Quilt Top Diagram** for placement.*

1. Sew 3 Churn Dash Blocks together to make Row. Make 3 Rows.

2. Sew Rows together to make **quilt top center**.

Adding the Borders

1. Matching centers and corners, sew **side** then **top/bottom inner borders** to quilt top center.

2. Matching centers and corners, sew **side** then **top/bottom outer borders** to quilt top center to complete Quilt Top.

Completing the Quilt

1. Follow **Quilting**, page 72, to mark, layer, and quilt as desired. My quilt is machine quilted with meandering quilting.

2. Refer to **Adding A Hanging Sleeve**, page 76, to make and attach a hanging sleeve, if desired.

3. Follow **Binding**, page 76, to bind quilt using **binding strips**. ✳

Quilt Top Diagram

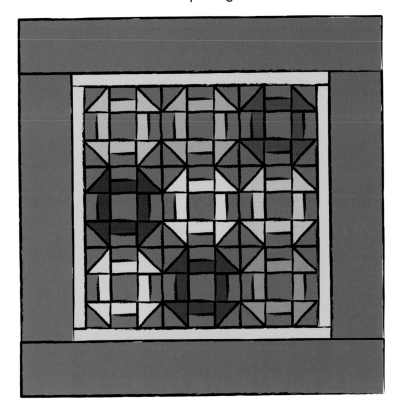

Fig. 1

Triangle-Square (make 4)

Strip Set

3¹/₂"

Unit 1 (make 4)

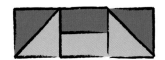

Unit 2 (make 2)

Unit 3

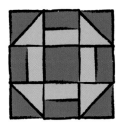

Churn Dash Block (make 9)

Row (make 3)

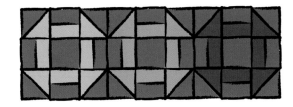

27

Cupcakes & Confections

With some novelty fabrics, there's just no need to explain what you like about them. This quilt is a way to always have sweet treats on hand and never gain a pound—if you don't let it inspire you to stop by the bakery or confectioner's! Of course, the design will work with any large-scale print that catches your eye. I think the polka-dot border fabric is perfect for playing up the rich brown of the chocolate candies, as well as the little blue squares formed as you sew the blocks together. The cupcakes are eye-catching all by themselves.

Finished Size: 53" x 61" (135 cm x 155 cm)
Finished Block Size: 8" x 8" (20 cm x 20 cm)

Fabric Requirements

Yardage is based on 43"/44" (109 cm/112 cm) wide fabric.

- $1^1/_8$ yds (1 m) of novelty print #1 (Snowball blocks)
- $^3/_8$ yd (34 cm) of novelty print #2 (Churn Dash blocks)
- $^1/_4$ yd (23 cm) *each* of 4 assorted pink/white prints (Churn Dash blocks)
- $^3/_8$ yd (34 cm) of pink print (inner border)
- $^3/_8$ yd (34 cm) of brown print (Churn Dash blocks)
- $1^1/_8$ yds (1 m) of brown dot print (outer border)
- $^1/_4$ yd (23 cm) *each* of 3 teal prints (Churn Dash and Snowball blocks)
- $^3/_8$ yd (34 cm) of 1 teal print (Churn Dash blocks, Snowball blocks, and outer border corner blocks)
- $^3/_8$ yd (34 cm) of teal dot print (binding)
- $3^7/_8$ yds (3.5 m) of fabric for backing

You will also need:

- 61" x 69" (155 cm x 175 cm) rectangle of batting

Cutting the Pieces

Follow Rotary Cutting, page 71, to cut fabric. Cut all strips from the selvage-to-selvage width of the fabric. Cutting lengths for borders are exact. All measurements include ¹/₄" seam allowances.

From novelty print #1:
- Cut 4 strips 8¹/₂"wide. From these strips, cut 15 **large centers** 8¹/₂" x 8¹/₂".

From novelty print #2:
- Cut 2 strips 4¹/₂"wide. From these strips, cut 15 **small centers** 4¹/₂" x 4¹/₂".

From *each* pink/white print:
- Cut 4 strips 1¹/₂" wide.

From pink print:
- Cut 2 top/bottom inner borders 1¹/₂" x 40¹/₂", piecing as necessary.
- Cut 2 **side inner borders** 1¹/₂" x 50¹/₂", piecing as necessary.

From brown print:
- Cut 3 strips 3" wide. From these strips, cut 30 **squares** 3" x 3".

From brown dot:
- Cut 2 top/bottom outer borders 5¹/₂" x 42¹/₂", piecing as necessary.
- Cut 2 **side outer borders** 5¹/₂" x 50¹/₂", piecing as necessary.
- Cut 2 large squares 6" x 6."

From *each* of 4 teal prints:
- Cut 1 strip 3" wide. From these strips, cut a *total* of 30 **squares** 3" x 3".
- Cut 1 strip 2¹/₂" wide. From these strips, cut a *total* of 60 **small squares** 2¹/₂" x 2¹/₂".
- From 1 of the 4 teal prints, cut 2 large squares 6" x 6".

From teal dot:
- Cut 6 binding strips 1¹/₂" wide.

Making the Blocks

*Follow **Piecing**, page 71, and **Pressing**, page 72, to make the Blocks. Match right sides and use ¹/₄" seam allowances throughout.*

CHURN DASH BLOCKS

1. Draw a diagonal line on wrong side of each teal **square**. With right sides together, place 1 marked teal square on top of 1 brown **square**. Stitch ¹/₄" from each side of drawn line (Fig. 1).

2. Cut along drawn line and press seam allowances toward darker fabric to make 2 Triangle-Squares. Trim each Triangle-Square to 2¹/₂" x 2¹/₂". Make 60 Triangle-Squares.

3. Sew 4 assorted pink/white print **strips** together to make Strip Set. Make 4 Strip Sets. Cut across Strip Sets at 2¹/₂" intervals to make Unit 1's. Make 60 Unit 1's.

4. Sew 2 Triangle-Squares and 1 Unit 1 together to make Unit 2. Make 30 Unit 2's.

5. Sew 2 Unit 1's and 1 **small center** together to make Unit 3. Make 15 Unit 3's.

6. Sew 2 Unit 2's and 1 Unit 3 together to make Churn Dash Block. Make 15 Churn Dash Blocks.

SNOWBALL BLOCKS

1. Place 1 teal **small square** on each corner of 1 **large center**. Stitch diagonally across each small square; trim ¹/₄" from stitching line (Fig. 2). Press open to make Snowball Block. Make 15 Snowball Blocks.

Fig. 1

Triangle-Square (make 60)

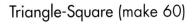

Strip Set (make 4)

Unit 1 (make 60)

$2^1/2"$

Unit 2 (make 30)

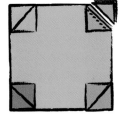

Unit 3 (make 15)

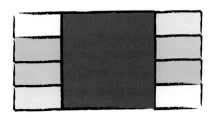

Churn Dash Block (make 15)

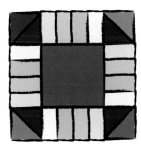

Fig. 2

Snowball Block (make 15)

Row 1 (make 3)

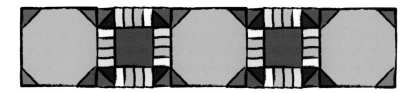

Row 2 (make 3)

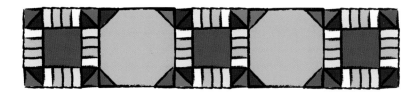

Fig. 3

Large Triangle-Square (make 4)

Top/Bottom Outer Border (make 2)

Assembling the Quilt Top

*Refer to **Quilt Top Diagram** for placement.*

1. Sew 3 Snowball Blocks and 2 Churn Dash Blocks together to make **Row 1**. Make 3 Row 1's.

2. Sew 2 Snowball Blocks and 3 Churn Dash Blocks together to make **Row 2**. Make 3 Row 2's.

3. Alternating Rows 1 and 2, sew Rows together to make **quilt top center**.

Adding the Borders

1. Matching centers and corners, sew **top/bottom** then **side inner borders** to quilt top center.

2. Draw a diagonal line on wrong side of each teal **large square**. With right sides together, place 1 marked teal large square on top of 1 brown dot **large square**. Stitch $1/4$" from each side of drawn line (Fig. 3).

3. Cut along drawn line and press seam allowances toward darker fabric to make 2 Large Triangle-Squares. Trim each Large Triangle-Square to $5^1/2$" x $5^1/2$". Make 4 Large Triangle-Squares.

4. Sew **side outer borders** to opposite sides of quilt top center.

5. Sew 1 Large Triangle-Square to either end of remaining 2 outer borders to make Top/Bottom Outer Borders.

6. Sew top/bottom outer borders to quilt top center to complete Quilt Top.

Completing the Quilt

1. Follow **Quilting**, page 72, to mark, layer, and quilt as desired. My quilt is machine quilted in the ditch between the blocks. There is a flower design in the Snowball blocks and in the diamonds formed at the intersection of the teal triangles. There are waves in the pink/white strips of the Churn Dash blocks and in the inner and outer borders.

2. Refer to **Adding A Hanging Sleeve**, page 76, to make and attach a hanging sleeve, if desired.

3. Follow **Binding**, page 76, to bind quilt using **binding strips**. ✳

Quilt Top Diagram

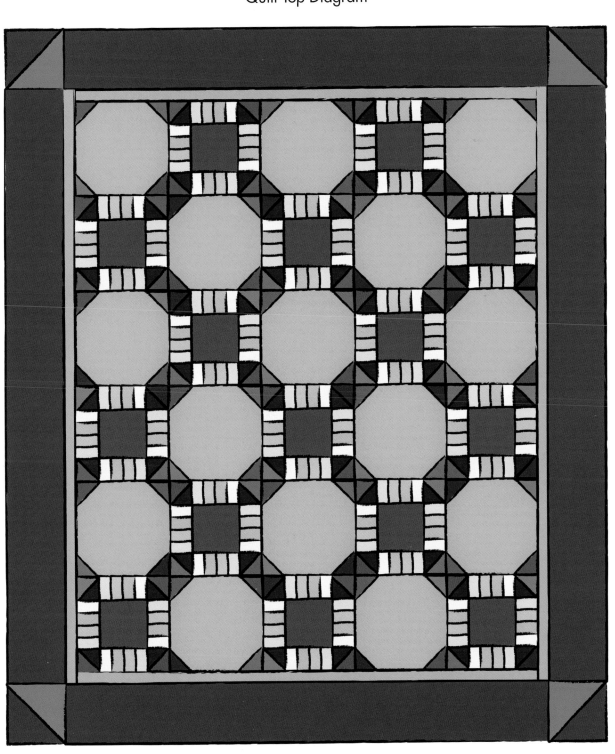

Doggie Adoration

It is no secret—I love dogs! I don't have any at the moment, but I love them dearly. A fabric that combines dogs, hearts, and words, well that is a great fabric! For this quilt, I wanted to show off a lot of the print. This design was just the thing, because it uses just the one novelty print very nicely.

Finished Size: 65" x 65" (165 cm x 165 cm)
Finished Block Size: 20" x 20" (51 cm x 51 cm)

Fabric Requirements

Yardage is based on 43"/44" (109 cm/112 cm) wide fabric.

$1^{1}/_{2}$ yds (1.4 m) of novelty print (blocks, sashings, and borders)*

1 yd (91 cm) of red print (blocks and sashings)

$^{3}/_{4}$ yd (69 cm) of red dot print (blocks and sashings)

$1^{1}/_{4}$ yds (1.1 m) of red stripe (outer border)

1 yd (91 cm) of black print (blocks, sashings, and binding)

1 yd (91 cm) of black gingham (blocks and borders)

$4^{1}/_{8}$ yds (3.8 m) of fabric for backing

You will also need:

73" x 73" (185 cm x 185 cm) square of batting

*When using a directional large print like the doggie fabric, I like to buy an extra $^{1}/_{2}$ yd so I can fussy cut the images I want to feature. Yardage given **does not** include that extra $^{1}/_{2}$ yd.

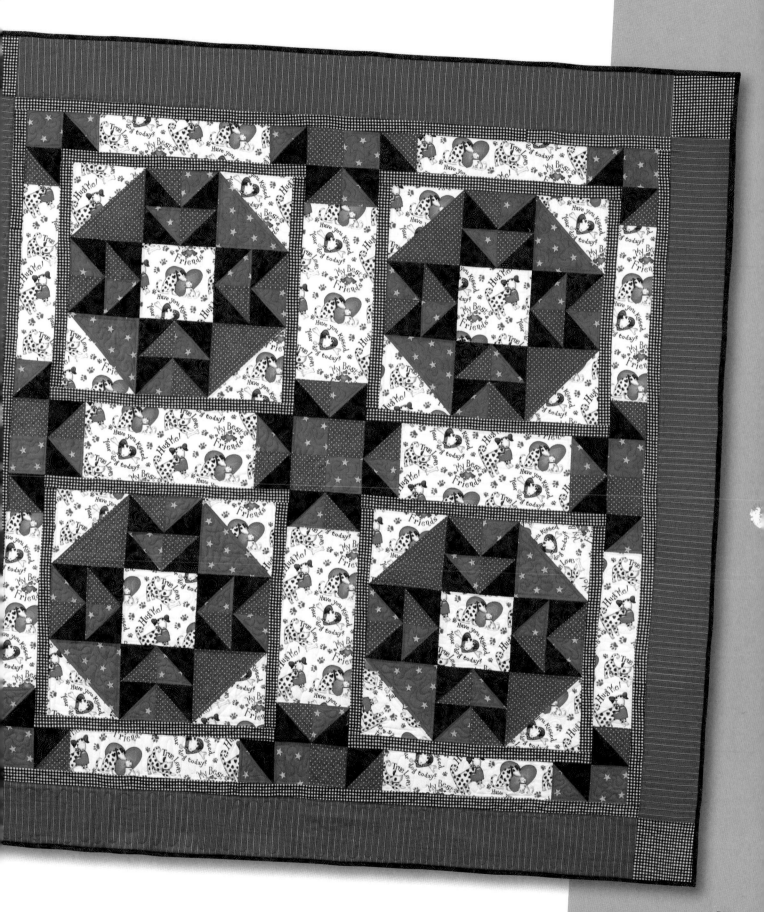

Cutting the Pieces

*Follow **Rotary Cutting**, page 71, to cut fabric. Cut all strips from the selvage-to-selvage width of the fabric. Cutting lengths for borders are exact. All measurements include $^1/_4$" seam allowances.*

From novelty print:
- Cut 2 strips 7" wide. From these strips, cut 8 **large squares** 7" x 7".
- Cut 2 strips $3^1/_2$" wide. From these strips, cut 4 **horizontal small rectangles** $14^1/_2$" x $3^1/_2$".
- Cut 2 strips $6^1/_2$" wide. From these strips, cut 4 **center squares** $6^1/_2$" x $6^1/_2$" and 2 **horizontal large rectangles** $14^1/_2$" x $6^1/_2$".
- Cut 1 strip $14^1/_2$" wide. From this strip, cut 4 **vertical small rectangles** $3^1/_2$" x $14^1/_2$" and 2 **vertical large rectangles** $6^1/_2$" x $14^1/_2$".

From red print:
- Cut 2 strips 7" wide. From these strips, cut 8 **large squares** 7" x 7".
- Cut 3 strips 4" wide. From these strips, cut 24 **squares** 4" x 4".
- Cut 1 strip $3^1/_2$" wide. From this strip, cut 10 **small squares** $3^1/_2$" x $3^1/_2$".

From red dot print:
- Cut 1 strip 7" wide. From this strip, cut 4 **large squares** 7" x 7".
- Cut 3 strips 4" wide. From these strips, cut 24 **squares** 4" x 4".
- Cut 1 strip $3^1/_2$" wide. From this strip, cut 6 **small squares** $3^1/_2$" x $3^1/_2$".

From red stripe:
- Cut 4 **outer borders** $5^1/_2$" x $54^1/_2$", piecing as necessary.

From black print:
- Cut 5 strips 4" wide. From these strips, cut 48 **squares** 4" x 4".
- Cut 7 binding strips $1^1/_2$" wide.

From black gingham:
- Cut 1 strip $5^1/_2$" wide. From this strip, cut 4 **corner squares** $5^1/_2$" x $5^1/_2$".
- Cut 8 strips $1^1/_2$" wide. From *each* strip, cut 1 **short strip** $1^1/_2$" x $18^1/_2$" and 1 **long strip** $1^1/_2$" x $20^1/_2$".
- Cut 2 **side middle borders** $1^1/_2$" x $52^1/_2$", piecing as necessary.
- Cut 2 **top/bottom middle borders** $1^1/_2$" x $54^1/_2$", piecing as necessary.

Making the Blocks

*Follow **Piecing**, page 71, and **Pressing**, page 72, to make the Blocks. Match right sides and use $^1/_4$" seam allowances throughout.*

1. Draw a diagonal line on wrong side of each novelty print **large square**. With right sides together, place 1 marked novelty print large square on top of 1 red **large square**. Stitch $^1/_4$" from each side of drawn line (Fig. 1).

2. Cut along drawn line and press seam allowances toward darker fabric to make 2 Triangle-Square A's. Trim each Triangle-Square A to $6^1/_2$" x $6^1/_2$". Make 16 Triangle-Square A's.

3. Repeat Steps 1-2 using 1 red print or red dot **square**, and 1 black **square** to make Triangle-Square B's. Trim each Triangle-Square B to $3^1/_2$" x $3^1/_2$". Make 96 Triangle-Square B's.

4. Sew 1 red print and 1 red dot Triangle-Square B together to make Unit 1. Make 40 Unit 1's. Set remaining Triangle-Square B's aside for sashings.

5. Sew 2 Unit 1's together to make Unit 2. Make 16 Unit 2's. Set remaining Unit 1's aside for sashings.

6. Sew 1 Unit 2 and 2 Triangle-Square A's together to make Unit 3. Make 8 Unit 3's.

7. Sew 2 Unit 2's and 1 novelty print **center square** together to make Unit 4. Make 4 Unit 4's.

8. Referring to **Star Block Diagram**, sew 2 Unit 3's and 1 Unit 4 together to make **block center**. Make 4 block centers.

9. Matching centers and corners, sew 1 **short strip** to opposite sides of 1 block center. Sew 1 **long strip** to top and bottom edges of block center to complete Star Block. Make 4 Star Blocks.

Fig. 1

Triangle-Square A (make 16)

Triangle-Square B (make 96)

Unit 1 (make 40)

Unit 2 (make 16)

Unit 3 (make 8)

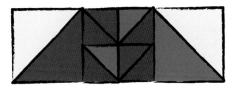

Unit 4 (make 4)

Star Block (make 4)

Unit 5

Unit 6 (make 2)

Unit 7 (make 2)

Row (make 2)

Sashing Row

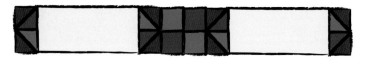

Assembling the Quilt Top

*Refer to **Quilt Top Diagram** for placement.*

1. Alternating red print and red dot, sew 4 red **small squares** together to make Unit 5.

2. Sew 1 Unit 1 to each end of 1 **horizontal large rectangle** to make Unit 6. Make 2 Unit 6's.

3. Sew 1 Unit 1 to each end of 1 **vertical large rectangle** to make Unit 7. Make 2 Unit 7's.

4. Sew 2 Star Blocks and 1 Unit 7 together to make Row. Make 2 Rows.

5. Sew 2 Unit 6's and 1 Unit 5 together to make Sashing Row.

6. Sew Rows and sashing row together to make **quilt top center**.

Adding the Borders

1. Sew 4 Triangle-Square B's, 1 red print small square, 1 red dot small square, and 2 **vertical small rectangles** together to make Side Inner Border. Make 2 side inner borders.

2. Sew 4 Triangle-Square B's, 3 red print small squares, 1 red dot small square, and 2 **horizontal small rectangles** together to make Top/Bottom Inner Border. Make 2 top/bottom inner borders.

3. Matching centers and corners, sew side, then top/bottom inner borders to quilt top center.

4. Matching centers and corners, sew **side**, then **top/bottom middle borders** to quilt top center.

5. Sew 2 **outer borders** to opposite sides of quilt top center.

6. Sew 1 **corner square** to either end of remaining **outer borders** to make Top/Bottom Outer Borders.

7. Sew top/bottom outer borders to quilt top center to complete Quilt Top.

Completing the Quilt

1. Follow **Quilting**, page 72, to mark, layer, and quilt as desired. My quilt is machine quilted with outline quilting around the triangles in the blocks and meandering quilting in the block backgrounds. There is outline quilting around the wide sashings and wavy lines through the centers. The middle and outer borders are quilted with wavy lines.

2. Refer to **Adding A Hanging Sleeve**, page 76, to make and attach a hanging sleeve, if desired.

3. Follow **Binding**, page 76, to bind quilt using **binding strips**. ✳

Side Inner Border (make 2)

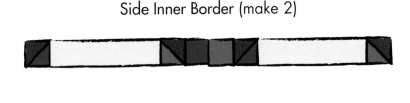

Top/Bottom Inner Border (make 2)

Top/Bottom Outer Border (make 2)

Quilt Top Diagram

island DreaMs

Sometimes, you go on vacation and pick up a bunch of fabrics that reflect the region—like, say, Hawaii! Now you have all these yummy prints but don't know what to do with them. I wanted a FAST quilt to show off these prints. They are 6" squares, which you can get from a fat quarter bundle, Layer Cake, or yardage. I set the squares together with a white-on-white fabric. You can use any tone-on-tone that fits your theme/color scheme; just keep it low-key so your squares stand out.

Finished Size: 48^1/$_2$" x 55^1/$_2$" (123 cm x 141 cm)

Fabric RequireMents

Yardage is based on 43"/44" (109 cm/112 cm) wide fabric.

20 assorted novelty print squares 6" x 6" (15 cm x 15 cm)

2^1/$_4$ yds (2.1 m) of white tone-on-tone print (sashings and borders)

^{3}/$_4$ yd (69 cm) of blue tone-on-tone print (setting strips, middle border, and binding)

3^1/$_2$ yds (3.2 m) of fabric for backing

You will also need:

56" x 63" (142 cm x 160 cm) rectangle of batting

Cutting the Pieces

Follow Rotary Cutting, page 71, to cut fabric. Cut all strips from the selvage-to-selvage width of the fabric. Cutting lengths for borders are exact. All measurements include ¹/₄" seam allowances.

From white tone-on-tone print:

- Cut 11 strips 2" wide. From these strips, cut 24 **short sashing strips** 2" x 6", 10 **medium sashing strips** 2" x 7¹/₂" and 5 **long sashing strips** 2" x 23".
- Cut 2 *lengthwise* **side inner borders** 2" x 39".
- Cut 2 *lengthwise* **top/bottom inner borders** 2" x 35".
- Cut 2 *lengthwise* **side outer borders** 6" x 44".
- Cut 2 *lengthwise* **top/bottom outer borders** 6" x 48".

From blue tone-on-tone print:

- Cut 4 strips 1¹/₂" wide. From these strips, cut 4 **short setting strips** 1¹/₂" x 7¹/₂", 2 **medium setting strips** 1¹/₂" x 16", and 2 **long setting strips** 1¹/₂" x 39".
- Cut 2 **top/bottom middle borders** 1¹/₂" x 37".
- Cut 2 **side middle borders** 1¹/₂" x 42", piecing as necessary.
- Cut 6 **binding strips** 1¹/₂" wide.

Assembling the Quilt Top

*Refer to **Quilt Top Diagram**, page 45, for placement. Follow **Piecing**, page 71, and **Pressing**, page 72, to make the Blocks. Match right sides and use ¹/₄" seam allowances throughout.*

Tip: Arrange your squares, sashing strips, and setting strips on a design wall or large flat surface until you are pleased with the placement of the squares, then take a photo for reference when piecing.

1. Sew 3 **squares** and 4 **short sashing strips** together to make Unit 1. Make 4 Unit 1's.

2. Sew 1 **long sashing strip** to the right side of 1 Unit 1 to make Unit 2.

3. Sew 1 **long sashing strip** to the left side of 1 Unit 1 to make Unit 3.

4. Sew 3 **long sashing strips** and 2 Unit 1's together make Unit 4.

5. Referring to **Unit Diagrams** for placement, sew 1 square, 1 short sashing strip, and 1 **medium sashing strip** together to make 1 each of Unit 5, 6, 7, and 8.

6. Referring to **Unit Diagrams** for placement, sew 2 squares, 2 short sashing strips, and 3 medium sashing strips together to make 1 of each Unit 9 and 10.

Unit 1 (make 4)

Unit 2

Unit 3

Unit 4

Unit 5

Unit 6

Unit 7

Unit 8

Unit 9

Unit 10

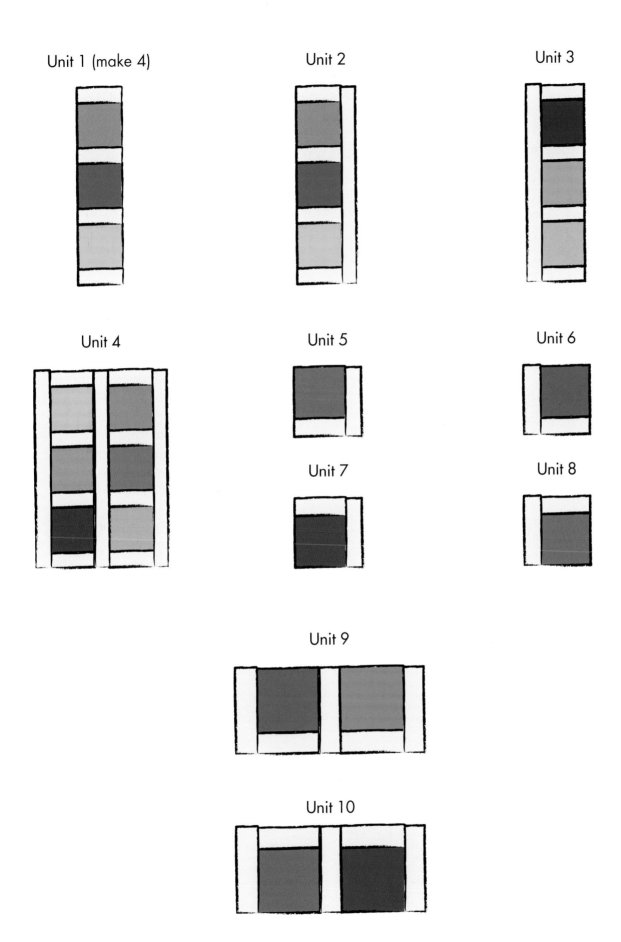

Row 1   **Row 2**

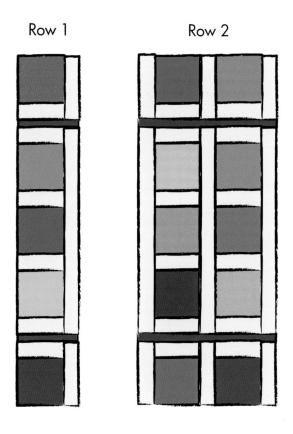

Row 3

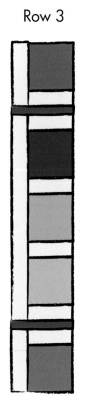

7. Sew Unit 5, Unit 2, Unit 7, and 2 **short setting strips** together to make vertical Row 1.

8. Sew Unit 9, Unit 4, Unit 10, and 2 **medium setting strips** together to make vertical Row 2.

9. Sew Unit 6, Unit 3, Unit 8, and 2 **short setting strips** together to make vertical Row 3.

10. Sew Rows 1-3 and 2 **long setting strips** together to make Quilt Top Center.

Adding the Borders

1. Matching centers and corners, sew **side** then **top/bottom inner borders** to quilt top center.

2. Matching centers and corners, sew **side** then **top/bottom middle borders** to quilt top center.

3. Matching centers and corners, sew **side** then **top/bottom outer borders** to quilt top center to complete Quilt Top.

Completing the Quilt

1. Follow **Quilting**, page 72, to mark, layer, and quilt as desired. My quilt is machine quilted with outline quilting around each block and along the setting strips. There is meandering quilting in the outer border and a wavy line through the center of the white inner border and sashing strips.

2. Refer to **Adding A Hanging Sleeve**, page 76, to make and attach a hanging sleeve, if desired.

3. Follow **Binding**, page 76, to bind quilt using **binding strips**. ✳

Quilt Top Center

Quilt Top Diagram

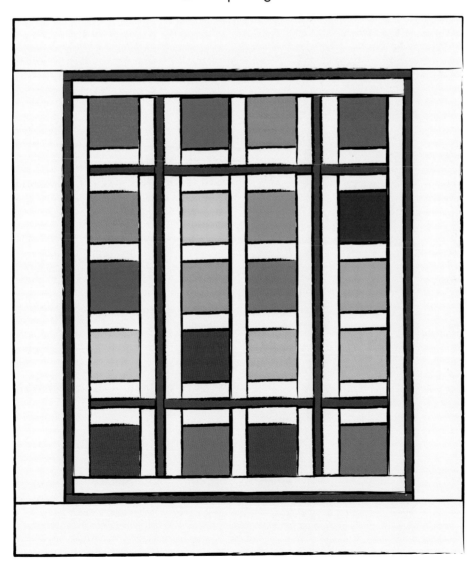

Let's Go Camping

This collection of novelty prints started with the chair fabric. My nana had these chairs on her front porch and I just love them. Her chairs were "that green" and she had a "davenport" too. When I really looked at this fabric line, I noticed all the scenes with families around their campers. What fun! My family didn't go on trips this way, but you know I might just have to! The quilt design is simple and quick. You can use a large-scale print and more than one print from the collection. Prints can be tossed or directional. And hey, if you want a bigger quilt, just make more blocks!

Finished Size: 49" x 49" (124 cm x 124 cm)
Finished Block Size: 10" x 10" (25 cm x 25 cm)

Fabric Requirements

Yardage is based on 43"/44" (109 cm/112 cm) wide fabric.

$^5/_8$ yd (57 cm) of green novelty print (setting blocks)

1 yd (91 cm) of green print (pieced blocks and Triangle-Squares)

$^3/_8$ yd (34 cm) *each* of 2 orange tone-on-tone prints (pieced blocks and Triangle-Squares)

$^3/_4$ yd (69 cm) of orange novelty print (corner squares, pieced blocks, Triangle-Squares, and binding)

$1^1/_4$ yds (1.1 m) of yellow novelty print (outer border)*

$3^1/_4$ yds (3 m) of fabric for backing

You will also need:

57" x 57" (145 cm x 145 cm) square of batting

* I used a directional print and cut *lengthwise* side borders. If you use a non-directional print and cut all borders *crosswise*, you will only need $^7/_8$ yd (80 cm).

Cutting the Pieces

Follow Rotary Cutting, page 71, to cut fabric. Cut all strips from the selvage-to-selvage width of the fabric. Cutting lengths for borders are exact. All measurements include $1/4$" seam allowances.

From green novelty print:
- Cut 4 setting squares $10^1/2$" x $10^1/2$".

From green print:
- Cut 2 side inner borders $1^1/2$" x $30^1/2$".
- Cut 2 top/bottom inner borders $1^1/2$" x $32^1/2$".
- Cut 4 strips $2^1/2$" wide. From these strips, cut 20 **rectangles** $2^1/2$" x $6^1/2$".
- Cut 3 strips 3" wide. From these strips, cut 32 **squares** 3" x 3".
- Cut 2 strips $2^1/2$" wide. From these strips, cut 20 **small squares** $2^1/2$" x $2^1/2$".

From orange novelty print:
- Cut 4 corner squares $6^1/2$" x $6^1/2$".
- Cut 2 strips $2^1/2$" wide. From these strips, cut 21 **small squares** $2^1/2$" x $2^1/2$".
- Cut 1 strip 3" wide. From this strip, cut 12 **squares** 3" x 3".
- Cut 6 binding strips $1^1/2$" wide.

From *each* orange tone-on-tone print:
- Cut 1 strip $2^1/2$" wide. From these strips, cut a *total* of 28 small squares $2^1/2$" x $2^1/2$".
- Cut 1 strip 3" wide. From these strips, cut a *total* of 24 squares 3" x 3".

From yellow novelty print:
- Cut 4 outer borders $6^1/2$" x $36^1/2$"*.

*If using a directional print, cut *2 lengthwise* and *2 crosswise* borders. If using non-directional print, cut all 4 borders *crosswise*.*

Making the Blocks

*Follow **Piecing**, page 71, and **Pressing**, page 72, to make the Blocks. Match right sides and use $1/4$" seam allowances throughout.*

1. Sew 1 green and 2 orange novelty or tone-on-tone print **small squares** together to make Unit 1. Make 10 Unit 1's.

2. Sew 1 orange novelty or tone-on-tone and 2 green print **small squares** together to make Unit 2. Make 5 Unit 2's.

3. Sew 2 Unit 1's and 1 Unit 2 together to make Unit 3. Make 5 Unit 3's.

4. Sew 1 **rectangle** to opposite sides of 1 Unit 3 to make Unit 4. Make 5 Unit 4's.

5. Sew 1 orange novelty or tone-on-tone print **small square** to each end of 1 **rectangle** to make Unit 5. Make 10 Unit 5's.

6. Sew 1 Unit 5 to top and bottom edges of 1 Unit 4 to make Block. Make 5 Blocks.

Assembling the Quilt Top

*Refer to **Quilt Top Diagram** for placement.*

1. Sew 1 **setting square** and 2 Blocks together to make Row 1. Make 2 Row 1's.

2. Sew 1 Block and 2 Setting Blocks together to make Row 2.

3. Alternating Rows 1 and 2, sew Rows together to make **quilt top center**.

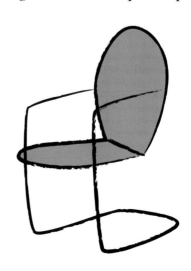

Unit 1 (make 10)

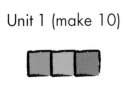

Unit 2 (make 5)

Unit 3 (make 5)

Unit 4 (make 5)

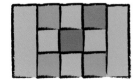

Unit 5 (make 10)

Block (make 5)

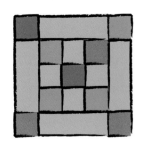

Row 1 (make 2)

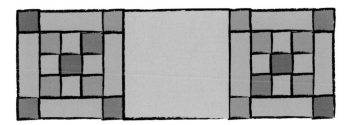

Row 2

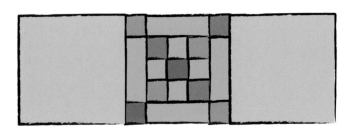

Fig. 1 Triangle-Square (make 64)

Middle Border (make 4) Top/Bottom Middle Border (make 2)

Top/Bottom Outer Border (make 2)

Quilt Top Diagram

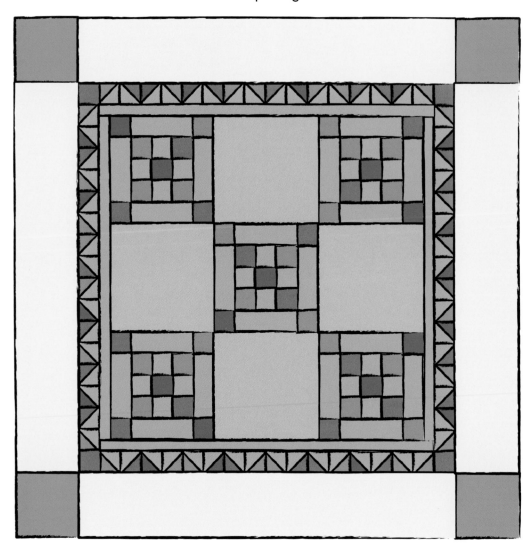

Adding the Borders

1. Matching centers and corners, sew **side** then **top/bottom inner borders** to quilt top center.

2. Draw a diagonal line on wrong side of each green print **square**. With right sides together, place 1 marked green square on top of 1 orange novelty or tone-on-tone print **square**. Stitch 1/4" from each side of drawn line (Fig. 1).

3. Cut along drawn line and press seam allowances toward darker fabric to make 2 Triangle-Squares. Trim each Triangle-Square to $2^1/_2$" x $2^1/_2$". Make 64 Triangle-Squares.

4. Sew 16 Triangle-Squares together to make Middle Border. Make 4 middle borders.

5. Sew 2 middle borders to opposite sides of quilt top center.

6. Sew 1 orange novelty or tone-on-tone print small square to either end of remaining 2 middle borders to make Top/Bottom Middle Borders.

7. Sew top/bottom middle borders to quilt top center.

8. Sew **outer borders** to opposite sides of quilt top center.

9. Sew 1 orange **corner square** to either end of remaining outer borders to make Top/Bottom Outer Borders.

10. Sew top/bottom outer borders to quilt top center to complete Quilt Top.

Completing the Quilt

1. Follow **Quilting**, page 72, to mark, layer, and quilt as desired. My quilt is machine quilted with loops and swirls in the outer border, the green triangles of the middle border, and block backgrounds. There are X's quilted in the orange squares of the blocks and outline quilting in the orange triangles of the middle border.

2. Refer to **Adding A Hanging Sleeve**, page 76, to make and attach a hanging sleeve, if desired.

3. Follow **Binding**, page 76, to bind quilt using **binding strips**. ❋

Monkey Business

The sock monkey fabric just keeps coming, and I think it's because we all love the classic toy! I had four prints from this line and added the black and yellow dot prints. The black squares show off the vertical lines and the yellow goes well with the bananas. I had only a limited amount of the banana fabric. If I had more of both novelty prints used in the blocks, I would have alternated the colors just for fun! You could use a directional fabric for the borders and background, but "tossed" prints seem to work better when the blocks are "on point."

Finished Size: 44" x 56$^1/_2$" (112 cm x 144 cm)
Finished Block Size: 6" x 6" (15 cm x 15 cm)

Fabric Requirements

Yardage is based on 43"/44" (109 cm/112 cm) wide fabric.
- $^1/_4$ yd (23 cm) of novelty print #1 (blocks)
- $^1/_2$ yd (46 cm) of novelty print #2 (blocks and binding)
- 1$^1/_2$ yds (1.4 m) of novelty print #3 (sashing strips and inner border)*
- 1$^5/_8$ yds (1.5 m) of novelty print #4 (setting triangles and outer border)
- $^1/_4$ yd (23 cm) of black dot print (blocks)
- $^1/_4$ yd (23 cm) of yellow dot print (blocks)
- 3$^5/_8$ yds (3.3 m) of fabric for backing

You will also need:
- 52" x 64" (132 cm x 163 cm) rectangle of batting

* I used a directional print and cut the top/bottom inner borders on the *crosswise* grain and the sashing strips and side inner borders on the *lengthwise* grain. If you use a non-directional print and cut all sashing strips and inner borders *crosswise*, you will only need $^1/_2$ yd (46 cm).

Cutting the Pieces

Follow Rotary Cutting, page 71, to cut fabric. Cut all strips from the selvage-to-selvage width of the fabric. Cutting lengths for borders are exact. All measurements include $1/4$" *seam allowances.*

From novelty print #1:
- Cut 2 strips $3^1/2$" wide. From these strips, cut 22 **squares** $3^1/2$" x $3^1/2$".

From novelty print #2:
- Cut 1 strip $3^1/2$" wide. From this strip, cut 8 **squares** $3^1/2$" x $3^1/2$".
- Cut 6 binding strips $1^1/2$" wide.

From novelty print #3:
- Cut 2 top/bottom inner borders $1^1/2$" x $31^1/2$".
- Cut 2 *lengthwise* side inner borders $1^1/2$" x 46".*
- Cut 2 *lengthwise* sashing strips $2^1/2$" x 44".*

From novelty print #4:
- Cut 2 strips $10^3/4$" wide. From these strips, cut 6 squares $10^3/4$" x $10^3/4$". Cut each square in half *twice* diagonally to make 24 **setting triangles.**
- Cut 1 strip 6" wide. From this strip, cut 6 squares 6" x 6". Cut each square in half *once* diagonally to make 12 **corner triangles.**
- Cut 2 top/bottom outer borders $5^1/2$" x $33^1/2$".
- Cut 2 side outer borders $5^1/2$" x 56", piecing as necessary.

From black dot:
- Cut 3 strips 2" wide.

From yellow dot:
- Cut 3 **strips** 2" wide.

* If using a non-directional print, cut all side inner borders and sashing strips crosswise, piecing as necessary.

Making the Blocks

*Follow **Piecing**, page 71, and **Pressing**, page 72, to make the Blocks. Match right sides and use* $1/4$" *seam allowances throughout.*

1. Sew 1 black dot and 1 yellow dot **strip** together to make Strip Set. Make 3 Strip Sets. Cut across Strip Set at 2" intervals to make Unit 1. Make 60 Unit 1's.

2. Sew 2 **Unit 1's** together to make Unit 2. Make 30 Unit 2's.

3. Sew 2 Unit 2's and 2 matching novelty print **squares** together to make Block. Make 15 Blocks.

Assembling the Quilt Top

*Refer to **Quilt Top Diagram** for placement. The corner and setting triangles are over-cut and will appear too large when assembling the units and rows. This allows the blocks to "float" when the sashing strips and inner borders are added.*

1. Aligning 1 **setting triangle,** 1 Block, and 1 **corner triangle** as shown, sew pieces together to make Unit 3. Make 6 Unit 3's.

2. Aligning 1 Block and 2 setting triangles as shown, sew pieces together to make Unit 4. Make 9 Unit 4's.

3. Sew 2 Unit 3's, 3 Unit 4's and 2 corner triangles together to make 1 vertical Row. Trim side seam allowances to $1/2$" and top/bottom seam allowances to $3/4$". Make 3 rows.

4. Sew 3 rows and 2 sashing strips together to make **quilt top center.**

Adding the Borders

*Refer to **Quilt Top Diagram** for placement.*

1. Matching centers and corners, sew **top/bottom** then **side inner borders** to quilt top center.

2. Matching centers and corners, sew **top/bottom** then **side outer borders** to quilt top center to complete Quilt Top.

Completing the Quilt

1. Follow **Quilting**, page 72, to mark, layer, and quilt as desired. My quilt is machine quilted with loops and swirls in the outer border. There are X's quilted through the centers of the small squares of the Blocks and a large asymmetrical wave in the Block backgrounds. The sashings and inner border have a wave through the center and are outline quilted.

2. Refer to **Adding A Hanging Sleeve**, page 76, to make and attach a hanging sleeve, if desired.

3. Follow **Binding**, page 76, to bind quilt using **binding strips**. ❋

Strip Set (make 3)   Unit 1 (make 60)   Unit 2 (make 30)

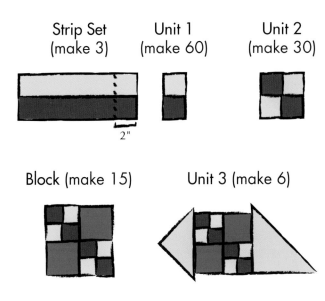

2"

Block (make 15)   Unit 3 (make 6)

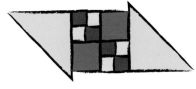

Unit 4 (make 9)

Quilt Top Diagram

Row (make 3)

Sailing, Sailing

When I saw this sailboat fabric, I just had to have it! I find it so relaxing to sit on the dock and watch beautiful boats on a summer day. This is what the fabric brings to mind. Also, this setting is perfect for that really large-scale print that you fall in love with. Make it with an animal print, children's print, or a scenery print. I went with a red/blue color scheme and I know just the man to give it to—someday!

Finished Size: 44" x 63" (112 cm x 160 cm)

Fabric Requirements

Yardage is based on 43"/44" (109 cm/112 cm) wide fabric.

$^3/_4$ yd (69 cm) of novelty print (wide strips)*

$^7/_8$ yd (80 cm) of navy blue print (sashings, borders, and binding)

$^1/_2$ yd (46 cm) of blue print (Triangle-Squares)

$^1/_2$ yd (46 cm) of light blue print (Triangle-Squares)

$^7/_8$ yd (80 cm) of red tone-on-tone print (Triangle-Squares)

4 yds (3.6 m) of fabric for backing

You will also need:

52" x 71" (132 cm x 180 cm) rectangle of batting

* I used a novelty print with a usable width of 42". An additional $^1/_4$ yard of fabric will be needed if your usable width is 40" or less.

Cutting the Pieces

Follow Rotary Cutting, page 71, to cut fabric. Cut all strips from the selvage-to-selvage width of the fabric. Cutting lengths for borders are exact. All measurements include ¹/₄" seam allowances.

From novelty print:
- Cut 3 wide strips 7¹/₂" x 40¹/₂", piecing as necessary.

From navy blue print:
- Cut 4 sashing strips 2" x 40¹/₂", piecing as necessary.
- Cut 2 top/bottom borders 2" x 40¹/₂", piecing as necessary.
- Cut 2 side borders 2" x 62¹/₂", piecing as necessary.
- Cut 6 binding strips 1¹/₂" wide.

From blue print:
- Cut 3 strips 5" wide. From these strips, cut 20 squares 5" x 5".

From light blue print:
- Cut 3 strips 5" wide. From these strips, cut 20 squares 5" x 5".

From red tone-on-tone print:
- Cut 5 strips 5" wide. From these strips, cut 40 squares 5" x 5".

Assembling the Quilt Top

Refer to Quilt Top Diagram for placement. Follow Piecing, page 71, and Pressing, page 72, to make the Blocks. Match right sides and use ¹/₄" seam allowances throughout.

1. Draw a diagonal line on wrong side of each blue print **square**. With right sides together, place 1 marked blue print square on top of 1 red tone-on-tone **square**. Stitch ¹/₄" from each side of drawn line (Fig. 1).

2. Cut along drawn line and press seam allowances toward darker fabric to make 2 Triangle-Square A's. Trim each Triangle-Square A to 4¹/₂" x 4¹/₂". Make 40 Triangle-Square A's.

3. Repeat Steps 1-2 using light blue print and red tone-on-tone squares to make 40 Triangle-Square B's.

4. Sew 10 Triangle-Square A's together to make Unit 1. Make 2 Unit 1's. Sew 10 Triangle-Square A's together to make Unit 2. Make 2 Unit 2's.

5. Sew 10 Triangle-Square B's together to make Unit 3. Make 2 Unit 3's. Sew 10 Triangle-Square B's together to make Unit 4. Make 2 Unit 4's.

6. Sew Units 1-4 together to make Unit 5. Make 2 Unit 5's.

7. Sew 3 **wide strips**, 2 Unit 5's, and 4 **sashing strips** together to make **quilt top center**.

8. Matching centers and corners, sew **top/bottom** then **side borders** to quilt top center to complete Quilt Top.

Completing the Quilt

1. Follow **Quilting**, page 72, to mark, layer, and quilt as desired. My quilt is machine quilted with an all-over wave and sailboat design.

2. Refer to **Adding A Hanging Sleeve**, page 76, to make and attach a hanging sleeve, if desired.

3. Follow **Pat's Binding**, page 76, to bind quilt using **binding strips**. ✳

Fig. 1

Triangle-Square A
(make 40)

Triangle-Square B
(make 40)

Unit 1 (make 2)

Unit 2 (make 2)

Unit 3 (make 2)

Unit 4 (make 2)

Quilt Top Diagram

Unit 5 (make 2)

Unit 1
Unit 3
Unit 4
Unit 2

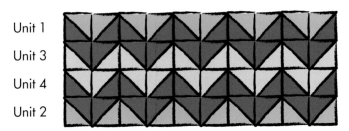

Panel Pizzazz

Oh, there are SO MANY great panel fabrics to dress up by adding multiple borders! I used wider inner borders on the top and bottom of my panel, but you may want the same width borders on all sides. The project instructions are for a panel that measures 19" x 23", but not all panels are the same size. Turn to page 63 to learn how to customize borders so they will fit your panel. It's easy and super effective—everyone will think you slaved for hours!

Finished Size: 34" x 40" (86 cm x 102 cm)
Finished Center Block Size: 19" x 23" (48 cm x 58 cm)

Note: Sizes, yardage, and instructions given are for the panel shown. Larger panels may require additional yardage for borders and backing while smaller panels may require less.

Fabric Requirements

Yardage is based on 43"/44" (109 cm/112 cm) wide fabric.
    1 novelty print panel (center block)
    $^3/_8$ yd (34 cm) of red print (checkerboard border and binding)
    $^1/_4$ yd (23 cm) of green print (checkerboard border)
    $^7/_8$ yd (80 cm) of green tone-on-tone print (inner and outer borders)
    $1^1/_2$ yds (1.4 m) of fabric for backing
You will also need:
    42" x 48" (107 cm x 122 cm) rectangle of batting

Cutting the Pieces

*Follow **Rotary Cutting**, page 71, to cut fabric. Cut all strips from the selvage-to-selvage width of the fabric. Cutting lengths for borders are exact. All measurements include $1/4$" seam allowances.*

From novelty print panel:
- Cut 1 center block 19$1/2$" x 23$1/2$".

From red print:
- Cut 2 strips 2$1/2$" wide. From these strips, cut 27 **squares** 2$1/2$" x 2$1/2$".
- Cut 4 binding strips 1$1/2$" wide.

From green print:
- Cut 2 strips 2$1/2$" wide. From these strips, cut 27 **squares** 2$1/2$" x 2$1/2$".

From green tone-on-tone print:
- Cut 2 side inner borders 2" x 23$1/2$".
- Cut 2 top/bottom inner borders 3" x 22$1/2$".
- Cut 2 side outer borders 4" x 32$1/2$".
- Cut 2 top/bottom outer borders 4" x 33$1/2$".

Assembling the Quilt

*Follow **Piecing**, page 71, and **Pressing**, page 72, to make the Blocks. Match right sides and use $1/4$" seam allowances throughout.*

1. Matching centers and corners, sew **side** then **top/bottom inner borders** to **center block** to make Unit 1.

2. Beginning with green and alternating colors, sew 7 red and 7 green **squares** together to make **side checkerboard border**. Make 2 side checkerboard borders.

3. Beginning with red and alternating colors, sew 7 red and 6 green **squares** together to make **top checkerboard border**.

4. Beginning with green and alternating colors, sew 6 red and 7 green **squares** together to make **bottom checkerboard border**.

5. Matching centers and corners, sew **side**, **top**, then **bottom checkerboard borders** to Unit 1 to make Unit 2.

6. Matching centers and corners, sew **side** then **top/bottom outer borders** to **Unit 2** to complete Quilt Top.

Completing the Quilt

1. Follow **Quilting**, page 72, to mark, layer, and quilt as desired. My quilt is machine quilted with leaves and swirls in the outer border, loops in the checkerboard border and leaves in the inner border. The Santa, elves, and "Jolly" are outline quilted. The background of the center block is quilted with a leaf and vine design.

2. Refer to **Adding A Hanging Sleeve**, page 76, to make and attach a hanging sleeve, if desired.

3. Follow **Binding**, page 76, to bind quilt using **binding strips**. ✱

Unit 1

Unit 2

Quilt Top Diagram

Borders

In order to attach the pieced border, the finished size of the quilt top center, after the inner borders are attached, must be an even number. This is achieved by adjusting the width of the inner borders. Simply follow the examples below and fill in the blanks with your numbers to determine the sizes to cut your borders.

1. Measure the width and height of your panel's design area. If the determined measurements are fractions, round up to the nearest whole number. The design area of our example measures 19" wide x 24" high, after rounding up.

Example:	My measurements:
Panel measures:	
19"w x 24"h	____w x ____h

2. The inner borders can be any width you desire as long as the combined finished size of the panel and inner borders is an even whole number. Add 3" *or more* to the panel measurements to obtain ***even whole*** numbers, keeping in mind that the added number is the *total finished width* of 2 inner borders.

Example:	My measurements:
19"w	____w
+3" for 2 side borders	+____for 2 side borders
22"	=____

24"h	____h
+4" for 2 top/bottom borders	+____for 2 top/bottom borders
28"	=____

3. To determine the *cutting width* of the inner borders, divide the *total finished width* from Step 2 by 2 and add $^1/_2$" for seam allowances.

Example:	My measurements:
Side inner borders:	
(3" ÷ 2 = 1$^1/_2$") + $^1/_2$" = 2"w.	____ ÷ 2 = ____ + $^1/_2$" = ____w

Example:	My measurements:
Top/bottom inner borders:	
(4" ÷ 2 = 2") + $^1/_2$" = 2$^1/_2$"w.	____ ÷ 2 = ____ + $^1/_2$" = ____w

4. To determine the *cutting length* of the side inner borders, add $^1/_2$" for seam allowances to the *height* measurement from Step 1. Cut side inner borders this length x the width measurement from Step 3.

Example:	My measurements:
Cut side inner borders:	
24$^1/_2$" long x 2"w	____long x ____wide

5. To determine the *cutting size* of the panel, add $^1/_2$" for seam allowances to the panel measurements from Step 1. Cut panel this size.

Example:	My measurements:
Cut panel:	
19$^1/_2$"w x 24$^1/_2$"h	____w x ____h

6. Sew side inner borders to panel. To determine the *cutting length* of the top/bottom inner borders, measure across the *width* of the panel *including* the side inner borders. Cut top/bottom inner borders this length x width measurement from Step 3. Sew top/bottom inner borders to panel.

Example:	My measurements:
Cut top/bottom inner borders:	
22$^1/_2$" long x 2$^1/_2$" wide	____long x ____wide

7. To cut the side pieced borders, measure the height of your quilt top center (including added borders) and divide by 2. This is the number of 2$^1/_2$" x 2$^1/_2$" squares you will need to cut for *each* side pieced border. *Note: You may wish to cut extra squares so you can audition placement for color choices.* Sew squares together to make 2 side pieced borders; sew borders to quilt top center.

Example:	My measurements:
28" ÷ 2 = 14	____ ÷ ____ = ____

8. Measure the width of your quilt top center (including added borders) and divide by 2. This is the number of 2$^1/_2$" x 2$^1/_2$" squares you will need to cut for *each* top/bottom pieced border. Sew squares together to make 2 top/bottom pieced borders; sew borders to quilt top center.

Example:	My measurements:
26" ÷ 2 = 13	____ ÷ ____ = ____

9. The outer borders can be any width you desire. Measure the height of your quilt top center (including added borders). Cut 2 side outer borders this measurement x the desired width. Sew side outer borders to quilt top center. Measure the width of your quilt top center (including added borders). Cut 2 top/bottom outer borders this measurement x the desired width. Sew top/bottom outer borders to quilt top center.

Quick Pillows

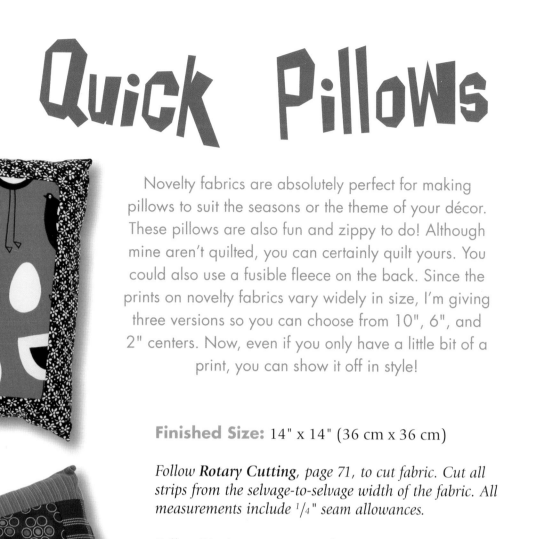

Novelty fabrics are absolutely perfect for making pillows to suit the seasons or the theme of your décor. These pillows are also fun and zippy to do! Although mine aren't quilted, you can certainly quilt yours. You could also use a fusible fleece on the back. Since the prints on novelty fabrics vary widely in size, I'm giving three versions so you can choose from 10", 6", and 2" centers. Now, even if you only have a little bit of a print, you can show it off in style!

Finished Size: 14" x 14" (36 cm x 36 cm)

Follow **Rotary Cutting**, *page 71, to cut fabric. Cut all strips from the selvage-to-selvage width of the fabric. All measurements include ¹/₄" seam allowances.*

Follow **Piecing**, *page 71, and* **Pressing**, *page 72, to make the pillows. Match right sides and use ¹/₄" seam allowances throughout.*

Fabric Requirements

Yardage is based on 43"/44" (109 cm/112 cm) wide fabric.

10½" x 10½" (27 cm x 27 cm) square of novelty print (center block)

½ yd (46 cm) of black print (borders and pillow back)

You will also need:

14" x 14" (36 cm x 36 cm) pillow form

Cutting the Pieces

From black print:

- Cut 2 strips 2½" wide. From these strips, cut 2 **top/bottom borders** 2½" x 14½" and 2 **side borders** 2½" x 10½".
- Cut 2 **pillow backs** 9¾" x 14½".

Chicken Pillow

Making the Pillow

1. Sew **side** then **top/bottom borders** to **center block** to complete Pillow Front.

2. Press 1 long edge of each **pillow back** ¼" to the wrong side twice. Topstitch hem close to the folded edges.

3. With right sides facing up, overlap the two hemmed edges of the pillow backs until the overall measurement is 14½" x 14½". Baste the overlapped edges together (Fig. 1).

4. Matching right sides, sew pillow front and back together. Clip corners and turn right side out. Insert pillow form to complete **pillow**. ❋

Pillow Front

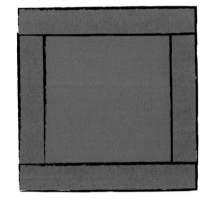

Fig. 1

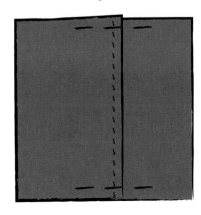

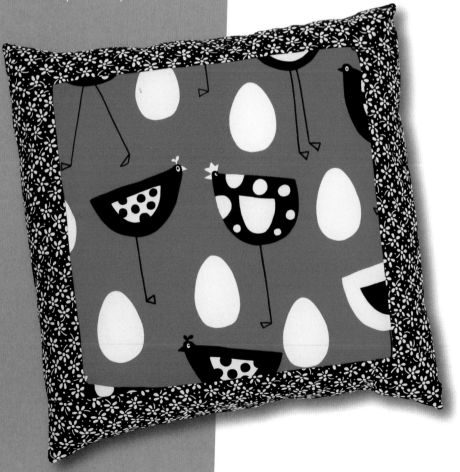

Fabric Requirements

Yardage is based on 43"/44" (109 cm/112 cm) wide fabric.

- $1/2$ yd (46 cm) of novelty print (center block, outer border, and pillow back)
- $1/8$ yd (11 cm) of green print (inner borders)

You will also need:

- 14" x 14" (36 cm x 36 cm) pillow form

Cutting the Pieces

From novelty print:

- Cut 2 strips $2^1/2$" wide. From these strips, cut 2 **top/bottom outer borders** $2^1/2$" x $10^1/2$" and 2 **side outer borders** $2^1/2$" x $14^1/2$".
- Cut 1 strip $9^3/4$" wide. From this strip, cut 2 **pillow backs** $9^3/4$" x $14^1/2$" and 1 **center block** $6^1/2$" x $6^1/2$".

From green print:

- Cut 1 strip $2^1/2$" wide. From this strip, cut 2 **top/bottom inner borders** $2^1/2$" x $6^1/2$" and 2 **side inner borders** $2^1/2$" x $10^1/2$".

Penguin Pillow

Making the Pillow

1. Sew **top/bottom** then **side inner borders** to center block.

2. Sew **top/bottom** then **side outer borders** to center block to complete Pillow Front.

3. Follow Steps 2-4 of **Making the Pillow**, page 66, to complete **pillow**. ✳

Pillow Front

Fabric Requirements

Yardage is based on 43"/44" (109 cm/112 cm) wide fabric.

- 6¹/₂" x 6¹/₂" (17 cm x 17 cm) square of novelty print (center block)
- ¹/₂ yd (46 cm) *total* of assorted blue prints, plaids, and stripes (borders and pillow backs)

You will also need:

- 14" x 14" (36 cm x 36 cm) pillow form

Cutting the Pieces

From assorted blue prints:

- Cut 2 **side inner borders** 2¹/₂" x 6¹/₂".
- Cut 2 **top/bottom inner borders** 2¹/₂" x 10¹/₂".
- Cut 2 **side outer borders** 2¹/₂" x 10¹/₂".
- Cut 2 **top/bottom outer borders** 2¹/₂" x 14¹/₂".
- Cut 2 **pillow backs** 9³/₄" x 14¹/₂".

Lunchbox Pillow

Making the Pillow

1. Sew **side** then **top/bottom inner borders** to center block.

2. Sew **side** then **top/bottom outer borders** to center block to complete Pillow Front.

3. Follow Steps 2-4 of **Making the Pillow**, page 66, to complete **pillow**. ❋

Pillow Front

SuMMertiMe Pillow

Fabric RequireMents

Yardage is based on 43"/44" (109 cm/112 cm) wide fabric.

- $^1/_8$ yd (11 cm) of novelty print (center block and 1 outer border)
- $^1/_2$ yd (46 cm) *total* of assorted pink prints and stripes (borders and pillow backs)

You will also need:
- 14" x 14" (36 cm x 36 cm) pillow form

Cutting the Pieces

From novelty print:
- Cut 1 center block $2^1/_2$" x $2^1/_2$".
- Cut 1 bottom outer border $2^1/_2$" x $14^1/_2$".

From assorted pink prints:
- Cut 2 side inner borders $2^1/_2$" x $2^1/_2$".
- Cut 2 top/bottom inner borders $2^1/_2$" x $6^1/_2$".
- Cut 2 side middle borders $2^1/_2$" x $6^1/_2$".
- Cut 2 top/bottom middle borders $2^1/_2$" x $10^1/_2$".
- Cut 2 side outer borders $2^1/_2$" x $10^1/_2$".
- Cut 1 top outer border $2^1/_2$" x $14^1/_2$".
- Cut 2 pillow backs $9^3/_4$" x $14^1/_2$".

Making the Pillow

1. Sew **side** then **top/bottom inner borders** to center block.

2. Sew **side** then **top/bottom middle borders** to center block.

3. Sew **side** then **top/bottom outer borders** to center block to complete Pillow Front.

4. Follow Steps 2-4 of **Making the Pillow**, page 66, to complete **pillow**. ✻

Pillow Front

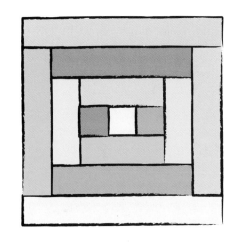

General instructions

To make your quilting easier and more enjoyable, we encourage you to carefully read all of the general instructions, study the color photographs, and familiarize yourself with the individual project instructions before beginning a project.

Fabrics

SELECTING FABRICS

Choose high-quality, medium-weight 100% cotton fabrics. All-cotton fabrics hold a crease better, fray less, and are easier to quilt than cotton/polyester blends.

Yardage requirements listed for each project are based on 43"/44" wide fabric with a "usable" width of 40" after shrinkage and trimming selvages. Actual usable width will probably vary slightly from fabric to fabric. Our recommended yardage lengths should be adequate for occasional re-squaring of fabric when many cuts are required.

PREPARING FABRICS

We recommend that all fabrics be washed, dried, and pressed before cutting. If fabrics are not pre-washed, washing the finished quilt will cause shrinkage and give it a more "antique" look and feel. Bright and dark colors, which may run, should always be washed before cutting. After washing and drying fabric, fold lengthwise with wrong sides together and matching selvages.

Rotary Cutting

Rotary cutting has brought speed and accuracy to quiltmaking by allowing quilters to easily cut strips of fabric and then cut those strips into smaller pieces.

- Place fabric on work surface with fold closest to you.

- Cut all strips from the selvage-to-selvage width of the fabric unless otherwise indicated in project instructions.

- Square left edge of fabric using rotary cutter and rulers (Figs. 1 - 2).

Fig. 1

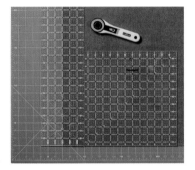

Fig. 2

- To cut each strip required for a project, place ruler over cut edge of fabric, aligning desired marking on ruler with cut edge; make cut (Fig. 3).

Fig. 3

- When cutting several strips from a single piece of fabric, it is important to make sure that cuts remain at a perfect right angle to the fold; square fabric as needed.

Piecing

Precise cutting, followed by accurate piecing, will ensure that all pieces of quilt top fit together well.

- Set sewing machine stitch length for approximately 11 stitches per inch.

- Use neutral-colored general-purpose sewing thread (not quilting thread) in needle and in bobbin.

- An accurate $1/4$" seam allowance is *essential*. Presser feet that are $1/4$" wide are available for most sewing machines.

- When piecing, always place pieces right sides together and match raw edges; pin if necessary.

- Chain piecing saves time and will usually result in more accurate piecing.

- Trim away points of seam allowances that extend beyond edges of sewn pieces.

SEWING STRIP SETS

When there are several strips to assemble into a strip set, first sew strips together into pairs, then sew pairs together to form strip set. To help avoid distortion, sew seams in opposite directions (Fig. 4).

Fig. 4

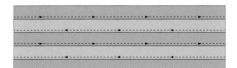

SEWING ACROSS SEAM INTERSECTIONS

When sewing across intersection of two seams, place pieces right sides together and match seams exactly, making sure seam allowances are pressed in opposite directions (Fig. 5).

Fig. 5

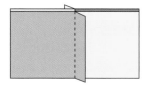

SEWING SHARP POINTS

To ensure sharp points when joining triangular or diagonal pieces, stitch across the center of the "X" (shown in pink) formed on wrong side by previous seams (Fig. 6).

Fig. 6

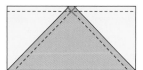

Pressing

- Use steam iron set on "Cotton" for all pressing.

- Press after sewing each seam.

- Seam allowances are almost always pressed to one side, usually toward darker fabric. However, to reduce bulk it may occasionally be necessary to press seam allowances toward the lighter fabric or even to press them open.

- To prevent dark fabric seam allowance from showing through light fabric, trim darker seam allowance slightly narrower than lighter seam allowance.

- To press long seams, such as those in long strip sets, without curving or other distortion, lay strips across width of the ironing board.

Quilting

Quilting holds the three layers (top, batting, and backing) of the quilt together and can be done by hand or machine. Because marking, layering, and quilting are interrelated and may be done in different orders depending on circumstances, please read entire **Quilting** *section, pages 72 – 75, before beginning project.*

TYPES OF QUILTING DESIGNS
In the Ditch Quilting

Quilting along seamlines or along edges of appliquéd pieces is called "in the ditch" quilting. This type of quilting should be done on side **opposite** seam allowance and does not have to be marked.

Outline Quilting

Quilting a consistent distance, usually $1/4$", from seam is called "outline" quilting. Outline quilting may be marked, or $1/4$" wide masking tape may be placed along seamlines for quilting guide. (Do not leave tape on quilt longer than necessary, since it may leave an adhesive residue.)

Motif Quilting

Quilting a design, such as a feathered wreath, is called "motif" quilting. This type of quilting should be marked before basting quilt layers together.

Crosshatch Quilting

Quilting straight lines in a grid pattern is called "crosshatch" quilting. Lines may be stitched parallel to edges of quilt or stitched diagonally. This type of quilting may be marked or stitched using a guide.

Meandering Quilting

Quilting in random curved lines and swirls is called "meandering" quilting. Quilting lines should not cross or touch each other. This type of quilting does not need to be marked.

MARKING QUILTING LINES

Quilting lines may be marked using fabric marking pencils, chalk markers, water- or air-soluble pens, or lead pencils.

Simple quilting designs may be marked with chalk or chalk pencil after basting. A small area may be marked, then quilted, before moving to next area to be marked. Intricate designs should be marked before basting using a more durable marker.

Caution: Pressing may permanently set some marks. **Test** different markers **on scrap fabric** to find one that marks clearly and can be thoroughly removed.

A wide variety of pre-cut quilting stencils, as well as entire books of quilting patterns, are available. Using a stencil makes it easier to mark intricate or repetitive designs.

To make a stencil from a pattern, center template plastic over pattern and use a permanent marker to trace pattern onto plastic. Use a craft knife with single or double blade to cut channels along traced lines (Fig. 7).

Fig. 7

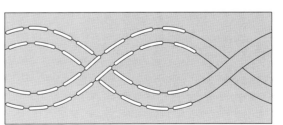

PREPARING THE BACKING

To allow for slight shifting of quilt top during quilting, backing should be approximately 4" larger on all sides. Yardage requirements listed for quilt backings are calculated for 43"/44"w fabric. To piece a backing using 43"/44"w fabric, use the following instructions.

1. Measure length and width of quilt top; add 8" to each measurement.

2. Cut backing fabric into two lengths slightly longer than determined *length* measurement. Trim selvages. Place lengths with right sides facing and sew long edges together, forming tube (Fig. 8). Match seams and press along one fold (Fig. 9). Cut along pressed fold to form single piece (Fig. 10).

Fig. 8   Fig. 9

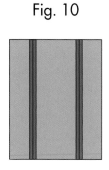

Fig. 10

3. Trim backing to size determined in Step 1; press seam allowances open.

CHOOSING THE BATTING

The appropriate batting will make quilting easier. For fine hand quilting, choose low-loft batting. All cotton or cotton/polyester blend battings work well for machine quilting because the cotton helps "grip" quilt layers. If quilt is to be tied, a high-loft batting, sometimes called extra-loft or fat batting, may be used to make quilt "fluffy."

Types of batting include cotton, polyester, wool, cotton/polyester blend, cotton/wool blend, and silk.

When selecting batting, refer to package labels for characteristics and care instructions. Cut batting same size as prepared backing.

ASSEMBLING THE QUILT

1. Examine wrong side of quilt top closely; trim any seam allowances and clip any threads that may show through front of the quilt. Press quilt top, being careful not to "set" any marked quilting lines.

2. Place backing *wrong* side up on flat surface. Use masking tape to tape edges of backing to surface. Place batting on top of backing fabric. Smooth batting gently, being careful not to stretch or tear. Center quilt top *right* side up on batting.

3. If machine quilting, use 1" rustproof safety pins to "pin-baste" all layers together, spacing pins approximately 4" apart. Begin at center and work toward outer edges to secure all layers. If possible, place pins away from areas that will be quilted, although pins may be removed as needed when quilting.

MACHINE QUILTING METHODS

Use general-purpose thread in bobbin. Do not use quilting thread. Thread the needle of machine with general-purpose thread or transparent monofilament thread to make quilting blend with quilt top fabrics. Use decorative thread, such as a metallic or contrasting-color general-purpose thread, to make quilting lines stand out more.

Straight-Line Quilting

The term "straight-line" is somewhat deceptive, since curves (especially gentle ones) as well as straight lines can be stitched with this technique.

1. Set stitch length for six to ten stitches per inch and attach a walking foot to sewing machine.

2. Determine which section of quilt will have longest continuous quilting line, oftentimes the area from center top to center bottom. Roll up and secure each edge of quilt to help reduce the bulk, keeping fabrics smooth. Smaller projects may not need to be rolled.

3. Begin stitching on longest quilting line, using very short stitches for the first $1/4$" to "lock" quilting. Stitch across project, using one hand on each side of walking foot to slightly spread fabric and to guide fabric through machine. Lock stitches at end of quilting line.

4. Continue machine quilting, stitching longer quilting lines first to stabilize quilt before moving on to other areas.

Free-Motion Quilting

Free-motion quilting may be free form or may follow a marked pattern.

1. Attach a darning foot to sewing machine and lower or cover feed dogs.

2. Position quilt under darning foot; lower foot. Holding top thread, take a stitch and pull bobbin thread to top of quilt. To "lock" beginning of quilting line, hold top and bobbin threads while making three to five stitches in place.

3. Use one hand on each side of darning foot to slightly spread fabric and to move fabric through the machine. Even stitch length is achieved by using smooth, flowing hand motion and steady machine speed. Slow machine speed and fast hand movement will create long stitches. Fast machine speed and slow hand movement will create short stitches. Move quilt sideways, back and forth, in a circular motion, or in a random motion to create desired designs; do not rotate quilt. Lock stitches at end of each quilting line.

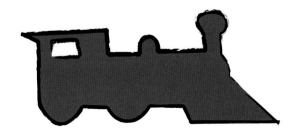

Adding a Hanging Sleeve

Attaching a hanging sleeve to the back of a wall hanging or quilt before the binding is added allows project to be displayed on wall.

1. Measure width of quilt top edge and subtract 1". Cut piece of fabric 7"w by determined measurement.

2. Press short edges of fabric piece $1/4$" to wrong side; press edges $1/4$" to wrong side again and machine stitch in place.

3. Matching wrong sides, fold piece in half lengthwise to form tube.

4. Before sewing binding to quilt, match raw edges and pin hanging sleeve to center top edge on back of quilt.

5. Bind quilt, treating hanging sleeve as part of backing.

6. Blindstitch bottom of hanging sleeve to backing, taking care not to stitch through to front of quilt.

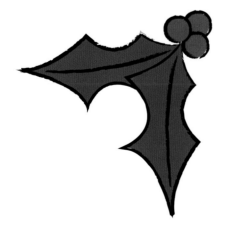

BLIND STITCH

Come up at 1, go down at 2, and come up at 3 (Fig. 11). Length of stitches may be varied as desired.

Fig. 11

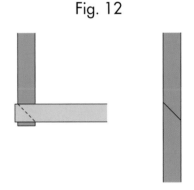

Binding
MAKING STRAIGHT GRAIN BINDING

1. With right sides together and using diagonal seams (Fig. 12), sew the short ends of the binding strips together to achieve the necessary length for each edge of quilt.

Fig. 12

2. Press seam allowances open. Press one long edge of binding $1/4$" to the wrong side.

PAT'S MACHINE-SEWN BINDING

For a quick and easy finish when attaching straight-grain binding, Pat sews her binding to the back of the quilt and Machine Blanket Stitches or Straight Stitches it in place on the front, eliminating all hand stitching.

1. Using a narrow zigzag, stitch around quilt close to the raw edges (Fig. 13). Trim backing and batting even with edges of quilt top.

Fig. 13

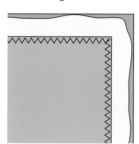

2. Beginning with one end near center on bottom edge of quilt, lay binding around quilt to make sure that seams in binding will not end up at a corner. Adjust placement if necessary. Matching raw edges of binding to raw edge of quilt top, pin binding to the backing side of quilt along one edge.

3. When you reach first corner, mark ¹/₄" from corner of quilt top (Fig. 14).

Fig. 14

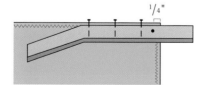

4. Beginning approximately 10" from end of binding and using a ¹/₄" seam allowance, sew binding to quilt, backstitching at beginning of stitching and at mark (Fig. 15). Lift needle out of fabric and clip thread.

Fig. 15

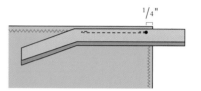

5. Fold binding as shown in Figs. 16 – 17 and pin binding to adjacent side, matching raw edges. When you've reached the next corner, mark ¹/₄" from edge of quilt top.

Fig. 16

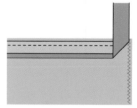

Fig. 17

6. Backstitching at edge of quilt top, sew pinned binding to quilt (Fig. 18); backstitch at the next mark. Lift needle out of fabric and clip thread.

Fig. 18

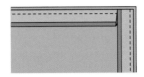

7. Continue sewing binding to quilt, stopping approximately 10" from starting point (Fig. 19).

Fig. 19

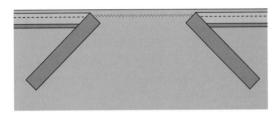

8. Bring beginning and end of binding to center of opening and fold each end back, leaving a $1/4$" space between folds (Fig. 20). Finger press folds.

Fig. 20

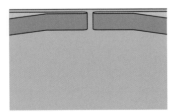

9. Unfold ends of binding and draw a line across wrong side in finger-pressed crease. Draw a line through the lengthwise pressed fold of binding at the same spot to create a cross mark. With edge of ruler at cross mark, line up 45° angle marking on ruler with one long side of binding. Draw a diagonal line from edge to edge. Repeat on remaining end, making sure that the two diagonal lines are angled the same way (Fig. 21).

Fig. 21

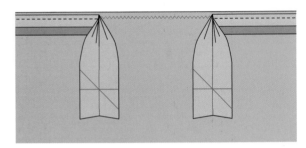

10. Matching right sides and diagonal lines, pin binding ends together at right angles (Fig. 22).

Fig. 22

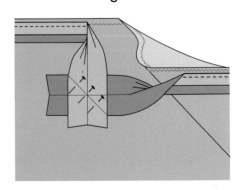

11. Machine stitch along diagonal line (Fig. 23), removing pins as you stitch.

Fig. 23

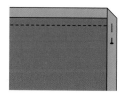

12. Lay binding against quilt to double check that it is correct length.

13. Trim binding ends, leaving a $1/4$" seam allowance; press seam open. Stitch binding to quilt.

14. On one edge of quilt, fold binding over to quilt front and pin pressed edge in place, covering stitching line (Fig. 24). On adjacent side, fold binding over, forming a mitered corner (Fig. 25). Repeat to pin remainder of binding in place.

Fig. 24   Fig. 25

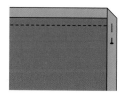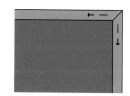

15. Blanket or Straight Stitch folded edge of binding to quilt front.

Signing & Dating Your Quilt

A completed quilt is a work of art and should be signed and dated. There are many different ways to do this and numerous books on the subject. The label should reflect the style of the quilt, the occasion or person for which it was made, and the quilter's own particular talents. Following are suggestions for recording the history of quilt or adding a sentiment for future generations.

- Embroider quilter's name, date, and any additional information on quilt top or backing. Matching floss, such as cream floss on white border, will leave a subtle record. Bright or contrasting floss will make the information stand out.

- Make label from muslin and use permanent marker to write information. Use different colored permanent markers to make label more decorative. Stitch label to back of quilt.

- Use photo-transfer paper to add image to white or cream fabric label. Stitch label to back of quilt.

- Piece an extra block from quilt top pattern to use as label. Add information with permanent fabric pen. Appliqué block to back of quilt.

- Write message on an appliquéd design from quilt top. Attach appliqué to back of the quilt.

Thanks to P&B Textiles, Andover Fabrics, Moda, and Robert Kaufman Fabrics for many of the beautiful fabrics featured in these projects and to Bernina for providing my sewing machine. To make the projects I used Aurifil® thread and Pellon® batting.

Metric Conversion Chart

Inches x 2.54 = centimeters (cm)	Yards x .9144 = meters (m)
Inches x 25.4 = millimeters (mm)	Yards x 91.44 = centimeters (cm)
Inches x .0254 = meters (m)	Centimeters x .3937 = inches (")
	Meters x 1.0936 = yards (yd)

Standard Equivalents

1/8"	3.2 mm	0.32 cm	1/8 yard	11.43 cm	0.11 m
1/4"	6.35 mm	0.635 cm	1/4 yard	22.86 cm	0.23 m
3/8"	9.5 mm	0.95 cm	3/8 yard	34.29 cm	0.34 m
1/2"	12.7 mm	1.27 cm	1/2 yard	45.72 cm	0.46 m
5/8"	15.9 mm	1.59 cm	5/8 yard	57.15 cm	0.57 m
3/4"	19.1 mm	1.91 cm	3/4 yard	68.58 cm	0.69 m
7/8"	22.2 mm	2.22 cm	7/8 yard	80 cm	0.8 m
1"	25.4 mm	2.54 cm	1 yard	91.44 cm	0.91 m